How They Met

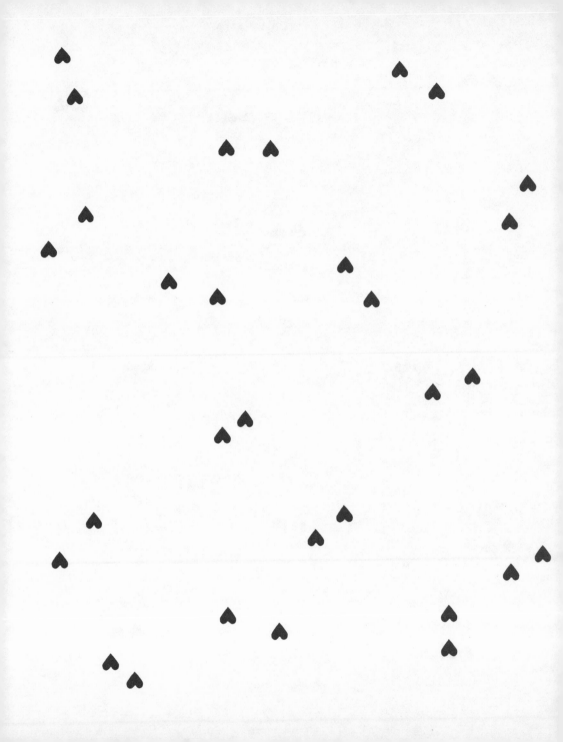

How They Met

Nancy Cobb

Turtle Bay Books

A Division of Random House

New York

1992

All rights reserved under International
and Pan-American Copyright Conventions.
Published in the United States by Turtle Bay Books,
a division of Random House, Inc.,
New York, and simultaneously in Canada
by Random House of Canada Limited, Toronto.

Library of Congress Cataloging-in-Publication Data
Cobb, Nancy.
How they met / Nancy Cobb
p. cm.
ISBN 0-679-40432-5
1. Courtship—United States.
2. Celebrities—United States.
3. Interpersonal attraction.
4. Mate selection—United States.
I. Title.
HQ801.A2C63   1992
306.73'4—dc20   91-75230

Manufactured in the United States of America

24689753

First Edition

Book design and illustrations by Peter Good

For my parents, Helen and Ted Cobb,
who couldn't live with or without each other.

As this book is a testament to relationships, so, too, is the process that formed it. Thus, much heartfelt appreciation goes to my husband, Geoffrey Drummond, and our daughter, Leland, for their unflagging enthusiasm and love; to my agent, Jonathan Dolger, for his constant support and good humor; to my publisher and editor, Joni Evans, for her energetic belief in this project from beginning to end, and to Susan Kamil for her editorial eye in between; to my friends Peter Good, for his particular ability to create just-right illustrations, Alice Mattison, for her generosity and keen brain, and Cordelle Kemper Ballard, who, at ninety-four, is, as ever, an inspiration.

Many thanks also go to Christina Gratz and Karen Rinaldi at Turtle Bay Books, to Suzie Akos and Mark Reiter at IMG, and to Les Crystal, Valerie Heller, Carol Matthau, Sarah Rockwell, Mary Rodgers, and Tamara Weiss for their varied and kindly efforts on my behalf.

And finally, a collective hug to all the couples inside these covers, for meeting . . . and telling.

Contents

When I was a child, a photograph of my parents at the Stork Club in an early stage of their courtship—forties-stylish, handsome, and clearly in love—captivated me. In retrospect, *that* they met was probably against all odds. She, a willowy fashion model, was a bookworm with a great wit. He, a former Ivy League football star, was a war hero back from overseas. His forebears came from England. Hers from Ireland. He was from Ithaca, she from Manhattan. Of the millions of possible meetings, fated, random, or arranged, theirs, each deciding at the last minute to attend a party that neither wanted to go to in the first place, still seems to me nothing short of miraculous. Or, at the very least, like a good movie.

In spite of my early and obvious bias, I still marvel over the fact that couples not only find each other, but manage to stay together, as my parents did, when the fur, and even a dish or two, flies. And though I realize now there are no guarantees, it's nice to know it can happen.

If I sound like Pollyanna, so be it. I am bored, TOTALLY (as my daughter would say), with adorable, ad-generated duos: eighteen and under, Nautilused, entwined eternally (or at least for the weekend), and clad in get-ups only slightly larger than their atten-

tion spans. Either the women look brainless and the men brawny or they all look like hermaphrodites. In the air-brushed face of nineties love, do real stories, in all their unpredictable imperfection, pale? I hope not. Because I believe these stories and the ritual of telling them give perspective and new energy to an old form: committed love.

Peggy Penn, a very fine half of one of my favorite couples and a director of the Ackerman Institute for Family Therapy, says she always asks married clients how they met, to understand what she calls their "original contract."

I like hearing about original contracts. No matter how stormy or serene the relationship, no matter how old or young the lovers, when couples tell their stories, when they recapture, even briefly, those first romantic feelings, their faces change, their eyes soften. It never fails. From my friends who met in a movie line in New York (a pediatrician and her husband), to my friends who met in a post-office line on Mykonos (she's American, he's Italian), to my dental hygienist, who met her husband between the Rice Krispies and the Corn Flakes (it was "singles night" at Stop & Shop, but she didn't know it), to a pair of smart, funny writers who met on the subway (IRT line, #6) . . . for all of them, the uncanny common thread is the look on their faces as they share their own sweet moment of recollection.

Okay, so I'm a diehard romantic. Now that I've gone public with it, I might as well add my own story to the collection.

Eleven years ago I met Geoffrey Drummond, an independent film producer, for a business lunch at Café des Artistes in New York. It was next door to his office, but it just so happens to be one of the most romantic restaurants in the city . . . low lights, deep banquettes, dark, richly paneled walls that frame Howard Chandler Christy murals—exquisite nudes (un-Nautilused) gamboling in sylvan settings—in the background. But never mind. In the

foreground we managed to talk business; a potential PBS series that my client would sponsor. Then the conversation changed abruptly, veered off, and took on a life of its own. We talked for the rest of the afternoon with no sense of time or place. And as we talked a seamless kind of geography unfolded, a terrain of past and present events, ideas, and people that were oddly familiar; known somehow. He made me laugh (his is a very dry humor), he was able to talk (without beating his chest), and he was quite handsome (dark and tall enough). Somehow, after that meeting, we both knew we would end up together. It was that simple. And though we certainly weren't kids (we had both been married, divorced, and were dating other people at the time), we felt like them. I can't tell you how or why it happened. You could call it serendipity, coincidence, timing. Or you could call it fate, like we do.

I hope the couples in this book delight, inform, and surprise the reader as much as they did me. But if they do nothing else than hold out the promise of possibility, I'll be satisfied. Because in the end, that's what love's about.

NANCY COBB
Guilford, Connecticut

How They Met

Place: New York City
Setting: Belasco Theatre
Time: August 21, 1955

It's almost impossible not to think of CAROL and WALTER MATTHAU as the odd couple. Odd and absolutely right. Carol, a tumble of blond curls in pink cashmere and ropes of rhinestones, has a little-girl breathiness that often gives way to a lower register and a lethal wit. Walter, in chinos, sweatshirt, and baseball cap, craggy-faced and gravel-voiced, is familiar and funny: wag, storyteller, intellect; everybody's uncle and nobody's fool.

"I got to the Belasco Theatre a day late for rehearsals for *Will Success Spoil Rock Hunter?* . . . had to be flown in by Army helicopter from the Pocono Playhouse because of floods. . . . Roads were washed out," says Walter, sounding a little like W. C. Fields. "Carol, who usually played the secretary, was understudying Jayne Mansfield the second day of run-throughs. She was lying on a massage table, and I, playing the part of the writer, was supposed to come in, pat her on the ass, and say, 'Rita, baby, how are ya?' The next day Jayne was back and I patted *her* ass. It felt like a handball court. So I asked George Axelrod, the director, if Carol could come back."

"I had made a date with George for lunch the following day. Then Walter asked if I'd have lunch with him," Carol remembers. "I thought he was terrific. There was something rugged and midwestern about him—all those hard *R*'s—" Walter gets a rascally look in his eye and is about to interrupt with the obvious, but Carol continues breezily. "—so I said, 'George, I'd rather go to lunch with Walter, okay?' "

"Did you really say that to him?" Walter asks.

"Yes, I did," Carol replies.

"How come I don't believe you?"

"Because you never believe me, ever."

"She used a dirty word at lunch, and I thought, if she's using that word, maybe I'll get lucky. Before I had the chance, she jumped me," Walter says with a laugh.

"Yes, I did, but that comes much later," Carol responds matter-of-factly. "George told me Walter was the best young actor in America, and that's true: He was, and is."

"You know, all the pictures where I played leading men made money," says Walter, changing the subject. "I guess people are really more interested in funny-looking fellas in the lead role."

"Who's funny-looking?" Carol stares at Walter stonily.

"Me," he replies.

"No," she says emphatically, "you're great-looking. . . ."

"Kinda funny-looking, big nose. . . ."

"You're great-looking, Walter, that's what I love about you. Nothing deep, just your looks . . . great voice, great-shaped head . . . you should see him when he's sleeping . . . adorable."

Every day after rehearsals Walter drove Carol to her mother's apartment at Park and Eighty-first, where she was staying during

the run of the play. She assumed he was on his way home until one day she discovered his address, posted on the Green Room bulletin board.

"It was Four-forty-four West Forty-fourth Street, right down the block from the Belasco!" Carol says. "I thought, oh, my, forty blocks, he likes me . . . a lot."

At the time Walter was married, though not happily, and there had already been several separations and reconciliations.

"The first time I saw his wife," Carol says, "our play was going on tour and she was seeing Walter off at the station. Her hair was in curlers. God, she was the other woman's dream."

Once in Philadelphia, Walter checked into the Warwick Hotel, and Carol, the Barclay.

"I had never had a one-night stand, and I wanted to be normal," she says. "So I put a raincoat over my nightie, walked to Walter's hotel, and slept with him."

What did Walter think? "You don't think at times like that," he says.

"That was the greatest thing that ever happened to me," says Carol.

"What do you mean?" Walter asks.

"I mean, it was so sensual, I thought I'd die. I went crazy. I couldn't think about anything else—"

"Carol, could you stop it? You're getting me excited—"

"—I would rather sit and wait for his call than be in Paris with anybody else," she interrupts. "You see, I'd been married to William Saroyan, twice, and it wasn't any fun, either time. People still say to me, 'You must have learned so much, living with Saroyan,' and I say, 'No, I didn't learn anything from him, but I have learned, and am still learning, from Walter.'

"I'm learning it all from you. I finally had the opportunity to test out my ideas and questions. You listened."

Carol and Walter each had two children to support as well as his ex-wife.

"I told him to give her everything because I'd rather be married to a poor man than a guilty one. But when he was poor *and* guilty, I got furious," Carol says, smiling, then adds, "He's the most romantic and tender man I've ever known. Before we met, everything was blurred. Now, each day, I take a minute to think where I am and what my life is about. I never did that before Walter."

Walter proposed to Carol by sending her a telegram. "I told the operator to write, "Darling, will you marry me?' The operator paused and said, 'Is that all?' I said, 'Isn't that enough?' "

They were married on August 21, 1959, four years, to the day, that they met.

Carol Matthau is a writer. *Walter Matthau* is an actor. They live in Los Angeles.

Place: Hudson, New York
Setting: Train Station
Time: Memorial Day Weekend, 1987

"He was with a very attractive woman," JIM HART says with a little smile, remembering the Sunday he bumped into Jake Brackman, an old friend, at the train station in Hudson, New York.

The woman was wearing gold sneakers and an enormous red shirt, belted and tucked into black-and-white-polka-dot pedal pushers. She was depressed . . . in a bad romance, not feeling her best and leaving Jake and Lila's house a day early, not wanting to "infect" them with her mood.

"I think he introduced us using first names only," Jim says. " 'Jim, this is Carly, Carly . . . Jim.' "

Before saying good-bye, Jake, CARLY SIMON's longtime friend and collaborator, whispered in her ear, "He's *major*," and Carly, though glum, took note. Praise from Jake came once in a blue moon.

Jim Hart, tall, lean, and dark, with merry Celtic eyes, has instant appeal. When he asked to join her in the virtually empty car, Carly couldn't resist. "I'd been reading about Grigori Orlov, Catherine the Great's first lover—an incredibly romantic figure, dark and Russian—and there was Jim, dark and Irish . . . close."

"We started up a traveling conversation," he says, "the kind where, because of the circumstances, there's an instant intimacy."

Carly remembers, "Jim held court. He was very candid, but he glossed over my small interjections, which I thought were quite provocative, as he told me the story of his life. He was attractive, in a seersucker sort of way . . . even a little nerdy. I couldn't figure him out. He had lots of literary connections, from his hometown and the Albany school of literature. He was a poet and a part-time businessman who wanted to be a novelist. He was different . . . and fascinating."

Toward the end of the ride Carly told Jim she was a singer.

"Oh, really," Jim replied. "My ex-wife is a singer. What kind of stuff do you sing?"

"Popular songs," she told him kindly. Silence. "Maybe you've heard of 'You're So Vain'? "

Jim nodded. It sounded familiar.

"She was reading Troyat's biography of Catherine the Great, and I told her she was pretty literate . . . for a singer." Jim winces a little as he remembers. "She said that her father had been a publisher; there were always lots of books around. . . ." More silence. Still no recognition.

"Okay, so I didn't make the Simon and Schuster connection. As for the song, it was old. Look, I thought maybe she was a folksinger," Jim protests. "What the hell was she doing on a train anyway? If she was a big rock star, why didn't she get a limo?"

Slowly, though, Jim began to make progress. She had either gone out with Jerry Brown or been married to James Taylor, right? (Carly confirms that Jim was not being "cute" and to this day quizzes him on popular music. "I've taught him to identify Marvin Gaye, Aretha, Stevie Wonder, the Rolling Stones . . . and Linda

Ronstadt . . . on the radio. He's improved. He gets it right about half the time.")

When they arrived at Grand Central Station, Carly, a bit miffed at Jim for monopolizing the conversation, said, "You know, you could ask some questions, too."

Seizing the opportunity to atone, Jim asked for a second chance. They made a date for dinner.

When she got home, Carly called her sister Lucy. "I met a man on the train. Remember *Moscow Does Not Believe in Tears?*"

Carly reminded Lucy of her deep connection to this film about a divorced woman with children, in her early forties, who meets a tall, handsome stranger on the train.

"I had seen it in 1982, but it stayed with me, kept floating back, and I somehow knew my life would imitate it. That's happened to me before with certain movies. . . . I latch on . . . make them part of me."

The following Monday, Jim mentioned that he had a date with "a" Carly Simon to a friend of his. When the friend, a bigtime fan of Carly's, came to, Jim realized what was up.

"Then," Jim says with a chuckle, "I thought, Hey, that was pretty slick, seducing Carly Simon, pretty slick."

Their first date was a dinner, family style, at Carly's West Side apartment with Jake and her children, Ben and Sally. Because they are an unusually close trio, it mattered greatly to Carly what her children thought of her new suitor.

"They both liked him. . . . Ben thought he was corny because he laughed at the silliest things, and Sally, probably because she had seen *Brigadoon* the night before, thought he looked like Gene Kelly. I, on the other hand, fell for something else," Carly says. "When he rolled up his trousers to show me an old knee injury, I

had a visceral reaction. It was a turning point . . . and a turn-on. I'm a fool for men's legs."

On their second date Jim read Carly his poem about their first meeting and *her* legs—in those red pants (they were black and white) and gold sneakers. He was sweet; she was touched and later wrote a song about him called "I Like a Man Who Fumbles Some."

"It took me awhile to get his sense of humor. His is goofy; mine is dry. He's like the man in the moon . . . smiling, laughing all the time." Carly pauses, then adds, "One night, though, when we were discussing Dylan Thomas, Jim became quite serious. As he talked, I realized I wasn't listening to anything he was saying. I was a planet in a gravitational force around him, the sun. It was a sort of weather condition, and I was in *his* atmosphere. That's the way it felt. That feeling grew, and like a magnet, I had to move closer. I had to jump."

"From the very beginning there was never any question that we'd be together forever," Jim says. "I think I proposed to Carly after five weeks."

Two days before Christmas, with the snow falling, they were married in a small church in Edgartown, Massachusetts.

"After what happened," Jim says, grinning, "I thought I should probably do an ad for Amtrak. You know, one of those 'look what happened to me on the train.' "

Carly Simon is a singer and writer. *Jim Hart* is a poet, at work on his first novel. They live in New York City and on Martha's Vineyard.

♥ ♥

Place: London, England
Setting: Old Vic Theatre
Time: 1938

BRENDA and ROBERTSON DAVIES could well have stepped from one of his own novels—say, *Fifth Business,* perhaps the most popular in his best-selling Deptford Trilogy. She, in a tailored suit, legs crossed at the ankle, and he, a cross between Father Christmas and Oxford don, weave their words mellifluously, drolly, with the give-and-take of a fifty-four-year bond.

"Tyrone Guthrie was directing a production of *A Midsummer Night's Dream* at the Old Vic in December of 1938. As well as teaching history of the theater at their school, I had a small part in the play. Brenda was the assistant stage manager," says Robertson Davies, looking and sounding very much like a part of theater history himself. "Tyrone wanted the curtain to come up at a very particular point near the end of the Mendelssohn overture, which was tricky. There were two endings, you see, and the first was false. If you counted the wrong bars, you could be in real trouble."

"It was my job to raise the curtain," Brenda recalls, "which was a bit of a problem. I couldn't read music. But I had seen Rob

counting bars during rehearsals and asked if he could help. He gallantly complied."

When World War II broke, the company began touring the small towns of England. Because of the blackout, returning to lodgings after an evening performance could be treacherous, particularly without a hard-to-come-by flashlight.

"Rob couldn't see well in the dark, so I used to help him find the way."

"My Seeing Eye," he says.

"So we had a reciprocal situation, a cooperation, which we've also had in our long marriage. We manage to fill the gaps in each other's blanks, as it were," Brenda says. "I think a community of interest is absolutely vital. Everybody talks about love as being so frightfully, frightfully important, but it must change as time goes on, become more supportive, more friendly, if you like. You must share things that both people take a deep interest in; otherwise it's boring."

"There's an awful lot of nonsense talked about love," he says. "You can't go on being married for over fifty years and keep love at one hundred eighty degrees Fahrenheit all the time. You've got to have a chance to think about something else. This notion that you sit around and adore one another is rubbish."

"It can't be done. The emphasis on sex is much too great, and the emphasis on relationship is not great enough," says Brenda.

"What keeps us going is a common interest in our children and grandchildren, the theater, music, and literature. . . . For instance, we're both great Shakespeare buffs, and it's amazing how Shakespeare will hold you together. There's so much to talk about, to think about," Robertson says.

"My graduate students used to say that they longed for old-

fashioned engagements," he continues, "instead of these shackup arrangements where there's so much examining and reexamining of feelings that you have to keep pumping up the love all the time."

"You have to give each other space, each person going his or her own way and bringing fresh interests to the joint relationship," she says.

"She can drive a car; I can't. I can spell; she can't," he says. They chortle, ensemble. "These are the things that balance off a relationship.

"During our courtship Brenda insisted on paying her own way every other time—extremely impressive, I thought. Most of the girls I knew would eat their weight in smoked salmon. It never occurred to them to pay for anything."

"I came from a broken home, so I was determined to have independence and a job of my own. I had no illusions about marriage," Brenda says. "Perhaps that's why I never took ours for granted."

Their union was not an ordinary one. She was Australian, and he Canadian. ("Both colonials of the British Empire, trying to pass as white in a place we didn't really belong," Robertson says.) When the war escalated, the Old Vic halted production altogether.

"We were both out of a job and had to decide whether to return to our respective countries or stay together and go to one place," Brenda recalls. "There was no time to dally about."

"Yes, it's true. We lost our jobs; there was a war on; everything looked black: This was obviously the time to get married."

And so they did, at the Chelsea Old Church, the actors' church, on the Embankment, in a small ceremony. Tyrone

. . . .

Guthrie—"Six-feet six inches, a fascinating Irishman with a terrific personality, one of the most beloved theater directors of all time"— gave the bride away. Then Brenda and Robertson Davies set off for Canada . . . colonials no more.

Brenda Davies is a former actress and ongoing theater buff. *Robertson Davies* is a novelist and professor. They live in Toronto.

Place: Buffalo, New York
Setting: A Cocktail Party
Time: 1955 (or was it '56?)

Take your pick: *The Dining Room, Love Letters,* or *The Cocktail Hour.*
MOLLY and PETE (A. R.) GURNEY are cut from the same WASP
cloth as the characters who lock jaws in his plays. But, though they
appear centrally cast, they work straight from the heart: no country-
club clichés; no need to grease the gab with martinis.

"Peter and I both grew up in Buffalo. As a matter of fact, our
parents were close friends. Buffalo is a big small town and—"

"—my mother actually married Molly's father [widow and
widower and onetime high school sweethearts!] years after we'd
been together."

"—we were both at a cocktail party in Buffalo in December
1956—" Molly continues.

"—given by a plump, affable widow," Pete adds.

"Actually, it might have been 1955. Was it 1955?"

"It would have been the spring of 1955. No. Spring of 1956. I
got out of the Navy and came home in '55. It was spring vacation."

"Spring?"

"Christmas?"

"There was the skating party after that. Remember?

"I guess you're right. . . . You may be right," he concurs.

"Okay. So it was December '55 or January '56. We immediately hit it off. Two weeks later I gave a skating party in Delaware Park, and then we all came back to my place for cocoa. After that we started to date. Peter was at Yale Drama School. We went out all that spring—"

"Summer," Pete suggests.

"That's right. We didn't start dating until June, when Peter came to New York on a J. Walter Thompson fellowship."

"I thought I was a hotshot, out of the Navy, in graduate school and working at the Kraft Television Theatre that summer, the same summer Molly dropped out of Bryn Mawr to work in New York."

"We began to date again. Neither one of us was making much dough, so we ate in cheap restaurants and took long walks."

"We'd go out to Jones Beach on weekends or just poke around town. New York was very romantic in the summer. I remember one night Molly asked me to come to her apartment so she could cook me dinner—square, premade hamburgers and frozen spinach— and I thought she was the most amazing and wonderful cook. Really extraordinary."

By the end of the summer Pete had proposed to Molly. She told him she would have to think about it.

"I was also interested in this doctor from the hospital where I was working, so I couldn't quite make up my mind."

"I wondered why Molly would always fall asleep on the way home from Jones Beach. As it turned out, this doctor was running a blood clinic. She'd go up and give blood all the time just to be near this guy."

"That's not quite true," Molly says, laughing.

"I was a man in a hurry. On Monday I called to declare myself once more. 'I know who you are and you know who I am. I think we should make our move and get married. Have you made up your mind?' and she said, 'Yes, I have. I don't want to marry you.' "

"No, I said, 'I still don't know. I'm still not sure.' I really wanted to go out with both of you."

That fall Pete, rebuffed, returned to drama school. Two months later, he relented, inviting Molly to Yale for the weekend.

"We fought," she says.

"Fighting can be very erotic. We fought, we made up . . . she fell into my arms. We were becoming very passionately involved, so I said, 'Now, come on, won't you please marry me?' And she said, 'Yes, I think I will.' "

"And we were, the following June 1957."

"One of the reasons I think we've stayed together is that melody that's been playing under our marriage and courtship: the city of Buffalo, the continuity, the fact that our parents were great friends, that we grew up with the same values, that we liked to do the same things."

It seems they still do.

Molly Gurney, mother of four grown Gurney children, is a nutritionist and volunteer tutor in the New York City school system. *A. R. Gurney* is a playwright and author.

♥♥

Place: Los Angeles
Setting: The Comedy Club/The Improv
Time: 1976

MAVIS and JAY LENO actually sound alike: similar speech patterns, similar timing. With tongue in cheek they approach life hand in glove, a bona fide team. Each is dark, one small, one large; each funny, and each the other's best fan. It's no surprise their sixteen-year marriage is a serious alliance.

In the mid-seventies Mavis Nicholson was writing comedy scripts with two partners. Tired of working on spec, she went to the newly opened Comedy Club one evening, hoping to beef up her chances of meeting story editors and producers.

"The whole comedy scene hadn't started yet because in those days everybody still wanted to be a rock star"—Mavis laughs—"so the club wasn't that crowded . . . with comics or audience.

"I was seated front row center, with my nose practically on the stage, in the middle of this guy's routine. I'd never heard of him, but he was funny, tall, and kind of cute, and after seeing some of the other acts, I realized just how good he was," she says.

The tall guy was a comedian named Jay Leno.

During intermission Mavis walked out of the ladies' room,

down a long hall where Jay and another comic, in the absence of a
Green Room, were talking. "Hi! Hey, wasn't that you, in the front
row?" Jay asked.

Mavis nodded and sailed by. "I barely spoke to him. I'm not
sure why," she says now. "He caught me by surprise, and when I
don't have time to anticipate, I'm shy. I also had a boyfriend at the
time. But I thought he probably would have been fun to know and
chalked it up as a lost opportunity."

The next week Mavis went to The Improv (at the time, the
other L.A. comedy club), which had an enormous plate-glass en-
tryway window. Looking in, she spotted a hat and thick black curls
floating above the crowd.

"Jay smoked a pipe, wore boots, which made him even taller,
and a snap-brimmed scoop-ace-reporter hat, over long ringlets.
The kind of hair most of us would die for," says Mavis. "When I
realized it was Jay, I thought, great . . . another chance."

This time a mutual acquaintance introduced them. They
talked, laughed, and became . . . friends.

"We were each seeing other people at the time," Mavis says.
"Jay was always very supportive. He was like that with
everybody—kind, helpful, easy to talk to—but even though we
were friends, there was always a little awkwardness, an underlying,
unspoken tension between us.

"As far as I knew, he was happy with his girlfriend, who was,
and is, a terrific person. On the other hand, I was nearing the end
of a relationship and had so much aggravation that I didn't need
any more."

Mavis remembers being astonished to discover that the day
she had ended her relationship, Jay had ended his.

Mavis, a self-confessed nineteenth-century Anglobibliophile,
created their modified English manor house and tucked it into a

lush Beverly Hills canyon, where it overflows with books: old and new, pop and profound, original editions and recycled paperbacks. You name it, Mavis has read it. And when she's not writing or reading, she's on the road with Jay, storing up material for a novel she's threatening to write.

"I always wanted to be an adventuress, like Colette or those *grandes horizontales* I had read about, minus the hooker aspect, of course," she says, removing her Clark Kent glasses to reveal gorgeous green eyes. "I was never much interested in marrying.

"Before Jay, I had been attracted to a particular type of man: highly neurotic, unrelentingly verbal, extremely volatile," she says. "I couldn't even envision having a relationship with Jay because he was their polar opposite. He was much more like me. We're two peas in a pod emotionally . . . v-e-r-y s-l-o-w. So it snuck up on me when I realized one day what had happened. I was in love with him."

Jay came to the same conclusion a bit before Mavis, and after they'd lived together for a year, he began to hint around about marriage, in spite of her views on the subject.

"From the time I was little, I always thought marriage was a sucker deal for women," says Mavis. "What was so wonderful about being a wife, this idealized goal for women . . . being supported? What kind of lazy idiot wants to sit around like a vegetable? Was I supposed to think it would be the ultimate life . . . to be Alice Cramden? In a cold-water flat, no money, no children; nothing to do but wait for your fat, loudmouthed husband to come home and sock you?

"Before Jay and I got together, I assumed I would never settle down. I couldn't imagine being with anyone forever. It was like I was always traveling, but as it turns out, there was a destination all along. . . . I just didn't know it. It was as if there was a party going

on somewhere and I couldn't get to it. Then, one day, I woke up and I realized, I'm at the party. . . . It's Jay; he's the party; he's the destination . . . and it was the goddamnedest feeling."

Mavis Leno is a writer. *Jay Leno* is a comedian and a host on *The Tonight Show*. They live in Los Angeles.

♥ ♥

Place: New York City
Setting: The Steps of Town Hall
Time: 1941

AGNES DE MILLE sits in her Greenwich Village apartment surrounded by books and papers, pencil behind her ear. She is tiny, eager, and tough, with an energy and a curiosity that belie her eighty-odd years. A nearby shelf is bowed from the weight of some of her own books: *To a Young Dancer, Where the Wings Grow, A Promenade Home, Dance to the Piper*, and *Reprieve*, which chronicles her comeback from a debilitating stroke in 1975. Almost twenty years later she maintains a daunting schedule, including hours of daily writing, which produced her most recent books, *Portrait Gallery*, a series of personal profiles, and *Martha: The Life and Work of Martha Graham*. Agnes de Mille, who has been called the "conscience of American dance," is, irrefutably, a national treasure.

"Martha Graham called me to invite me to a Ralph Kirkpatrick concert. And she told me to wear my prettiest dress because WALTER PRUDE was coming. I didn't want to be rude, but I said, "Who the hell is Walter Prude?' " Agnes recalls.

Then wonder eclipsed wariness. "It struck me when I first saw Walter on the steps of Town Hall before the concert. He was a nice

combination of Gary Cooper and George the Sixth . . . very handsome . . . and as it turned out, he knew a great deal about music.

"Afterwards we began to spar, so to speak, at the Blue Ribbon
Café, and two days later he came for tea. We continued to argue
and talk, with great excitement. He was tall and witty; he had an
elegance about him, a witty elegance. It was just eighteenth-century
. . . noblesse. And funny, funny, funny. He made me laugh.

"Days later he told me he had received greetings from the
president. I said, 'Oh, Walter, how wonderful.'

" 'Agnes,' he replied, 'that means I've been drafted.'

"When he went off to training camp, we had only known each
other two weeks. For the next year I became a camp follower, a
single groupie of sorts, visiting him at various Army bases around
the country. He finally ended up, a lieutenant, stationed in Omaha,
Nebraska."

Her visits to Walter were always brief. She was choreograph-
ing a new show, a musical, that was to preview in New Haven.

"I called him from the lobby of the Shubert Theatre there,"
she remembers, "where *Oklahoma!* had just opened. He asked when
I was coming out, and I told him, 'In three weeks, with luck.' 'Why
so long?' he wanted to know. Moments before, Richard Rodgers
and I had decided we just might have a hit, that it was bound to
open in New York."

After three weeks of hard work they did open in New York,
and the rest is history. But five days later Agnes managed to leave
Oklahoma! for Omaha.

"My leading dancers saw me off. Joan McCracken gave me an
old-fashioned bouquet, and Katharine Sergava, a magnum of Pommery," Agnes says, pausing, as if to recapture the moment at the
station.

"I presented the champagne to Walter at the end of my long

journey. I thought we should open it then and there, but he thought it wasn't quite the right moment."

A few days later, when they were having drinks at twilight, Walter proposed.

"I burst into tears, and he said, 'What's the matter with you? This isn't the first time someone has asked you to marry him, is it?' I said, 'No, but it's the first time I've said yes.'

"He had reserved a table at the most beautiful restaurant in Omaha, where the Pommery was on ice. 'I *wondered* what happened to that,' I said. 'I guess you took it for granted that I'd marry you.' "

"Yes," he said, "I guess I did."

Agnes de Mille is a choreographer and writer. *Walter Prude* was the general manager of the Hurok Organization for thirty years.

Place: Washington, D.C.
Setting: Howard University Campus
Time: 1949

One advantage to being the mayor of New York City—these days maybe the only advantage—is Gracie Mansion. This stately, pale yellow Federal house with views of the East River, formal gardens, and the only sizable, real-live lawn in all of Manhattan, is more evocative of the turn of the century than of the end of it, standing second only to its occupants, JOYCE and DAVID DINKINS, as a solid and symbolic shelter in the midst of a storm.

"During our courtship we used to drink beer in a place with red checkered tablecloths and talk about the future. I always promised Joyce a house in the country with a white picket fence," he says with a grin, "but, hey, this ain't bad."

The Dinkinses are a gentle and handsome couple who beam at the very mention of their son, daughter, or grandchildren. David even goes so far as to pull their well-worn photos from his breast pocket and display them with pride. Simply put, they're family folk who go back a long way.

"I think we were destined to meet," David Dinkins says in a

25

brief moment away from his grueling schedule. "What else could it be? When you figure how many people there are in the world . . . that two of them meet and stay together for almost forty years . . . it's destiny. It fits. After a certain length of time a long marriage just fits. Like a name. Take Efrem Zimbalist, Junior, for example. He couldn't be called John or Bob now . . . it wouldn't seem right."

Hizzoner spotted his bride-to-be, Joyce Burrows, when he was a senior and she a freshman at Howard University in the fall of 1949.

"I was lying on the grass, minding my own business, reading a calculus book, when she walked by," the soft-spoken mayor recalls. "And . . ." he adds with a smile, "she had great legs. You couldn't miss them."

"He stopped reading, looked up at me, and said, 'Freshman, what are you doing on the Senior Walk?' " Joyce Dinkins, as soft spoken as her husband, says almost shyly. "I was terrified . . . but I was also impressed. After all, he *was* reading a calculus book. I thought, 'He's not only a senior, he's a genius.' Later I found out he had been in the armed services and knew everyone on campus . . . as an underclassman, I was thrilled that he took the time to talk to me."

The senior asked the freshman for a date. She accepted readily and in short order they fell in love.

"He was very romantic," Joyce says. "I thought he was marvelous. And so, by the way, did my mother."

For the next four years, they dated as often as was possible, given that David was working in New Jersey and Joyce was still a student in Washington. David maintains, however, that he visited her enough to outdo the "other guys."

So Joyce didn't go out with anyone else?

"Well . . . I wouldn't say that . . . " she admits with a smile, "but I think I always knew that, in the end, my vote would go with David."

Joyce Dinkins is the first lady of New York City. *David Dinkins* is the mayor. And that's where they live.

♥♥

Place: New York City
Setting: Penthouse Apartment
Time: December 1967

RUTH and FRED FRIENDLY are a rarity: a couple who lives together, works together, *and* stays together. Their large family, an amalgam of off- and off-offspring from first marriages, is a unified and affectionate hybrid, bound in part by the same humor that underscores the marriage.

In the spring of 1967 Ruth Mark, a tall, slim redhead and a fifth-grade teacher with three teenage sons, became a widow. The following December Helen Bernstein called to say there was someone she really wanted her to meet. Helen had arranged a dinner party for eighteen people in their friend Claudette Colbert's Fifth Avenue apartment, which Helen and her husband, Bob, then chairman of Random House, often sublet around the holidays.

"The party was scheduled for December eleventh, nine months to the day after my husband's death. Lots of wonderful people were there: Bennett Cerf, Kitty Carlisle, Henry Dreyfuss, Ted Geisel (Dr. Seuss), and, of course, Bob and Helen. I was sitting there in my little blue dress when Fred came in," Ruth recalls. "He evidently said in a very loud voice, though I didn't hear him, 'You've

brought me here to meet someone!' to which Bob and Helen replied, simultaneously and respectively, *'No!'* and *'Yes!'*"

"Bob had called me a couple of weeks earlier and said, 'How 'bout having dinner with Helen and me on the eleventh?' and I assumed it would be just the three of us. When I arrived, I realized what was up. Glaring at Helen, I said, 'You fixed me up with a blind date, didn't you?' " he says in his inimitable Uncle-Fred-goes-for-the-jugular-ese.

Helen, the matchmaking culprit, confessed.

"After the party," says Fred, "I drove Ruth home to Scarsdale in my red Mustang. When we got to her front door, I told her I had enjoyed the evening and hoped to see her again. She looked up, with a kind of sad, plaintive expression on her face. . . . I leaned over and kissed her on the cheek and said, 'I assure you, my intentions are strictly honorable.' And she said, 'Let's set the date.' "

"That's a little made up," Ruth says, "the 'Let's set the date.' "

The story of what followed that night was told almost a year later at Thanksgiving, when Michael, Ruth's son and one of the six in their newly merged family (Fred also had three children from his previous marriage), asked Fred how he had proposed to his mother. Here's what Fred told him: "Bob Bernstein said, 'Fred, this is Ruth Mark, and Ruth, this is Fred Friendly.' Then, Fred swears he said, 'Hello Ruth. Will you marry me?' And when the kids heard this, they all cheered.

"It's like *Rashomon*," says Fred. "Two versions."

"At least. They've become our catchphrases over the years. Fred actually used 'My intentions are honorable' all the time. I thought it was a nice nineteenth-century phrase—"

"Victorian," Fred counters.

"Victorian," Ruth concedes.

"Edwardian," Fred parries.

"Edwardian . . . old-fashioned . . . What did you mean anyway?" Ruth lunges, laughing.

"It was bold of me to kiss you on the cheek. But it was a euphemism. . . ."

"Of course, I never said, 'Let's set the date.' "

"Why did you have it engraved on my watch then?"

"Fred, that came along well after we were married and—"

"Isn't that watch upstairs?"

"Stories evolve in this family . . . even after twenty-two years," Ruth says, adding one last significant detail, this time undisputed by her spouse. "Fred was quoted in *Newsweek* shortly before we met, saying, '. . . the newsroom and the classroom are moving closer and closer together.' Little did we know that two weeks later it would come true."

Fred Friendly, former president of CBS News, is the Edward R. Murrow professor of broadcast journalism at Columbia University and the creator/moderator of the PBS series of panel shows presenting dialogues ranging from the *Power of the Press* to *The Right to Die. Ruth Friendly*, a former teacher, is the show's producer.

♥ ♥

Place: New York City
Setting: Studio 54
Time: 1979

In the old days SPALDING GRAY sat at a battered table in SoHo's Performing Garage, allowing his conscious and unconscious to merge and flake over his loyal following, clustered in the bleachers. Today, with his monologues mainstreamed (*Swimming to Cambodia, Monster in a Box, Terrors of Pleasure*), Spalding seems to have rejuvenated, even reinvented, the soliloquy. With this in mind, picture a lean man in a plaid flannel shirt, eyes darting, mind racing, unfolding the story of boy meets girl.

"In 1979 I was given a SoHo Newspaper Arts Award for best performance of the Wooster Group's production of *Nyatt School*. There was a reception afterwards at Studio 54. Now, I'd never been to Studio 54—I don't think a person at the awards ceremony had ever been to Studio 54—but we were all to have two hours in the club before the 'regulars' arrived. Of course, we had to go in through the back door, but there was still the requisite line and the doorman . . . the very large doorman. He was doing this big power trip, letting the people in very slowly, one at a time and only if they had invitations.

"When it was my turn I said, 'Wait a minute, I don't have my invitation.'

"So he said, 'Get lost.'

"I said, 'Hey, I got an award, I got a sweater and everything . . .' wondering why I wanted to go in there in the first place.

"Two people behind me said, 'Look, you don't even know who you're talking to. That's Spalding Gray, he got an award!' Then they turned to me and said, 'Here, Spalding, take our invitations. We don't want to go into this shithole anyway.'

"So, like the begging dog I was at the time, I went in.

"I wandered around and danced with a few women . . . until I saw RENÉE. She had such an alive face, a great face, full of joy, sensuality. . . . It was incredibly open. I didn't even notice her body. We danced and talked; I tried to dance close, but she didn't seem to want to. I tried to keep my eye on her but she ran off—disappeared—like Cinderella.

"She had told me she managed a theater that showed experimental films. There were only two in New York at the time, so I figured it was the Collective for Living Cinema on White Street. I went there. I found her. Sitting behind an enormous desk. I liked that. She was even more attractive with all that power seated behind that large desk. I could see she was really in control of her life.

"I said, 'Why did you run away that night at Studio 54?'

"She said, 'Because I thought you were married and I didn't want to get involved.'

" 'No, no, no, no, no, no, no, no, no,' I said. 'I *was* living with a woman for twelve years but we're-not-together-now-so-you-shouldn't-be-threatened-will-you-have-dinner-with-me?'

"We went downtown to Mickey's Bar, where Belushi used to hang out, for our first date. Renée's Jewish, so she doesn't have a great tradition of drinking in her life, like I do. She mixed all the

wrong drinks: a brandy alexander and a kirsch and something else.

"Afterwards we went back to her apartment, which was in a semiconverted office building on John Street in lower Manhattan. She was feeling very insecure about it, convinced that Wall Street was going to crash any minute because they were renting out all these offices as apartments. She rambled on about it . . . I think she was a little drunk from all those different drinks. Then we were naked. We started to make love. I was on top of her when she said, 'Excuse me, but I think I'm going to throw up.'

"She couldn't make it to the bathroom, which was out in the hall, so I ran around and found an old metal Le Creuset cooking pot and made it back just in time. She threw up in the pot while I held her. I think she was so impressed that I stuck by her that it became the special thing that sealed our relationship. We've been together ever since."

Renée Shafransky is a writer and director. *Spalding Gray* is an actor and writer. They live in New York and, when they have to, California.

♥ ♥

Place: London
Setting: Book Party
Time: 1975

Imagine what would happen if RUTH and DAVID MACAULAY chucked it all and moved to Hollywood. Think of it. *Motel of the Mysteries, Cathedral, City, Pyramid*—his popular, whimsically written and illustrated best-selling classics—coming to full and glorious life as a year's worth of television miniseries. This is high-concept stuff— archaeological passion plays, sizzling on-screen, week after week. But after hearing the Macaulays' story, one knows 'tis infra dig to consider. In their case, happily, it's just not *The Way Things Work*.

"My London firm received a book from an American publisher called *Cathedral*," Ruth recalls. "It looked wonderful and so did the picture of the fellow who wrote it. Since I edited and published historical nonfiction, David was assigned as my author."

Their first contact was a written badinage, as it were, over the historically correct construction of a sunscreen in David's book *City*.

"I hadn't even seen Ruth. She had at least seen my photo-

graph. But it was a joy to receive her letters and fun to respond. Beyond that, I had nothing but curiosity," David says.

"I was in London on November fifth, 1975, Guy Fawkes night. I remember, because on the way to a book party from the tube stop, fireworks were going off everywhere. In retrospect, that seems quite apropos.

"There I was, being entertained royally, when Ruth and her husband arrived. I found her quite attractive . . . but it was a pretty wild and well-lubricated dinner. . . . She didn't actually slide under the table but—"

"Close to it. I was taking antibiotics and was not supposed to drink," she confesses.

"For the next few months we kept up the correspondence, and in the summer of '76 I went to Europe to do some research on castles," David recalls. "Coincidentally, we were both in the process of separating from our original spouses, but it had nothing to do with our knowing each other."

"He was rather mournful, so we all tried to cheer him up when he was in London. I was particularly sensitive because I was going through the same thing. One day we went out to lunch and told each other our sad stories."

"Yes, it was pathetic," David says.

"Heartrending," Ruth remembers.

"But we drank a lot of wine, and after a while it didn't seem so bad. Things were looking up. It's great when you have something in common like that."

"I was to go off with my former husband on summer holiday, one of those 'Let's see if we can work it out' vacations. We couldn't."

"The correspondence got increasingly suggestive after that,"

David recalls. "You know, if this is what's happening for me and that's what's happening for you, why don't we get together again and see if there's anything to work with?"

Cut to the spring of '77. A castle . . . in Dorset . . . and a group of philosophers from Oxford, plus one. Ruth.

"I had just separated from my husband and decided to go on this walking tour. In the evening they played these awful parlor games, terribly intellectual, which I loathed, so I left and met David."

"Yes, and I was there playing Monopoly and occasionally Scrabble. . . . Oh, I can't pretend anymore. I went to Dorset to see Ruth—and also to meet her parents."

"But he was still 'my author,' and at the time I was not interested in getting too involved with anybody. I was a little suspicious of David even though he tried to cover his tracks."

"I'm much more aggressive, obvious," says David.

"He came to my parents' house for dinner clutching two bottles of Asti Spumante, which they love. I thought, Two bottles, not one . . . typical ostentatious American. [David was born in the U.K. but raised in the U.S.] My parents did not share my opinion, however. Rather, they thought, Whoopee! Two bottles of wine!"

"Oh, yes, I got to them really quickly. It was a brilliant campaign."

"They adored you."

"Actually I think they were just desperate for a normal guy after all those philosophers. They thought I was really wholesome. Little did they know. . . ."

"At Thanksgiving we visited my friend's parents, Sir John and Lady Benn, in Surrey. She called and asked, 'One bedroom or two?'

"I wasn't quite sure, so she said she'd make up the double bed in one room and the single bed in the other and told me there was a door connecting the two, saying, 'You can do whatever you want to, dear.'

"When we arrived, there were logs for the fire, food in the oven, a bottle of wine on the table, and a note telling us to enjoy ourselves, they would be back quite late. It was incredibly romantic. . . . Lady Benn had planned the whole thing. When we went upstairs, the heat was on in the room with the double bed and off in the other."

"The following spring I visited Ruth in England and proposed to her in a taxi on the way from the airport. Quickly."

"Very quickly. He said something like 'I can't kidnap you, I can't import you, so I'll have to marry you.'"

"Terribly romantic. Actually I proposed again in the Rose Revived, an inn with a pub, near Oxford. At the bar. Now that I think of it, there was a lot of beer and wine consumed during this whole process."

"Including our wedding, where we ran around the park, popping champagne corks."

"There was a best woman and a best woman. . . . I was surrounded by women," David says with a grin, and adds, "I guess it was a long 'correspondence courtship,' but we actually only spent six weeks together before getting married."

"It's amazing to go back and read the letters. They were very flirtatious and funny," Ruth says. "We've saved most of them."

"Yes, but we had them bronzed, so they're kind of hard to read now."

*   *   *

Place: Baltimore, Maryland
Setting: The Giant (a supermarket)
Time: 1979

It can't be easy being married to former Baltimore Orioles pitching star JIM PALMER. Not only is he tall and drop-dead handsome, but every woman in America has seen him in his Jockey shorts. And if that ad campaign's not enough, he's a member of the Baseball Hall of Fame, a successful sportscaster, a devoted father, a funny guy, a nice guy, and a bright guy. Sigh. How does JONI PALMER handle the guy?

"We knew each other before, in another time, another place. I'm sure of it," she says, her personality instantly and infinitely larger than her lithe five-foot-two-inch frame. "I keep telling him that I know him better than he knows himself."

"And I tell her that if she keeps telling me that, I'll believe it," Jim says with a grin.

"I can finish his sentences for him."

Joni Pearlstone, a flash of freckles and brown hair, was never much of a baseball fan. But she was a good cook, a photographer,

a divorced mother living with her young son in the summer of 1979. The summer of the dinner party that changed her life.

"It was for my friends, Suki and Eddie, who had just gotten married. Suki was a big Jim Palmer fan and went to all the Orioles games when the team was in town, including the one on the eve of the party. They had invited me but I had too much to do. Later, Suki called from the stadium, breathless, ecstatic, to tell me what I was missing. Palmer had come off the disabled list in the fifth inning to pitch and the crowd had gone wild—gave him a standing ovation—and she wished I could be there. I told her I couldn't—I still hadn't bought fruit for tomorrow's pies and . . ."

Jim cuts in. "When was the last time we had home-baked pie?"

"What kind would you like?" Joni asks.

"Something a little more spontaneous."

"Just tell me what kind . . ."

"Blueberry, apple . . ."

"Okay."

"But, I don't *eat* pie anymore, Joni."

When the laughter ends Joni keeps going.

"After I got off the phone I did a few things and then went to The Giant [the local twenty-four-hour supermarket] around eleven or eleven-thirty. (I'm a late-night person.) I was standing near the entrance, beside the fruits and vegetables, when the door swung open and Jim Palmer walked in. I thought, This is crazy . . . and then I went over to him and said, 'You don't know me but I know you got a standing ovation tonight and I wasn't even there. You do know the friend [Jim had met Suki socially on several occasions] who called to tell me about it, though, and I'm having a party for

her tomorrow night. I'd love you and your wife to come . . . as a surprise.' "

He said, "I have a game tomorrow night." She said, "Come after the game."

He said he'd try. She gave him directions. They bumped into each other again in two other aisles—in one, he asked her where vacuum-cleaner bags were; she hadn't a clue—and finally ended up in the same checkout line.

The next evening Joni told everyone, except Suki, about the secret guest. In the middle of dinner, someone turned on the Orioles game to get the final score.

"They had gone into overtime," Joni explains.

Jim corrects her. "Extra innings, dear."

"Extra innings, right . . . extra innings," she says, chuckling.

As it got later and people began to leave, Joni decided to tell Suki about the botched surprise.

"I said, 'Suki, I had this present for you—it was a great idea— but I'm afraid it's not going to happen.' "

Once she heard the "Giant" story, however, Suki was not about to give up so easily. She grabbed Joni's hands, looked deeply into her eyes, and said, "Joni, let's concentrate. Let's put all of our energy together and will him to be here."

With that the doorbell rang. It was Jim Palmer. (His wife was out of town.)

A few weeks after the party, Joni obtained a coveted press pass to photograph one of the Orioles' final games. As it happened, the game was rained out, turning the next night's game, when Jim was pitching, into a doubleheader. Armed with a rain check, Joni took pictures of the first game. When it was over, the Orioles learned from the scoreboard that Milwaukee had lost,

which meant the Orioles were the American League Eastern Division champions.

"Corks were popping, champagne was flowing, and the next thing I knew, I was in the men's locker room," Joni remembers, "sitting in Earl Weaver's office reloading my camera, when suddenly I was surrounded by baseball players, who grabbed me, picked me up, carried me to the whirlpool, and dumped me in. That was the night I became a true Orioles' fan."

Joni and Jim discovered they had more in common than the same grocery store: skiing, tennis, raquetball, great love for their children (his two daughters are now in their twenties; her son's seventeen), and first marriages that ended in divorce, hers complete, his in process. So Joni, long before she became romantically involved with Jim, served as tennis partner and confidante during a very difficult time.

After they went beyond the confidante stage they "dated" for a decade, not marrying until April 1990, so today they're still virtually newlyweds. Why such a long courtship?

"Jim is very slow, very methodical about making decisions and commitments. But I'm very quick. Once I fell for him, I wouldn't let him out of the house. I'd put my shoes [size seven] inside his [size fourteen] and then, when he couldn't get them on and was helpless with laughter, I'd hide his keys.

"A friend of his told me, early on, that if I was going to get together with Jim Palmer, it was going to take forever. But after ten years I told Jim that I was definitely not going to wait around for another ten."

"Jane Silverman gave a toast at our wedding," Jim says, "that went something like this: 'To Joni—who made the longest journey of her life, from the plums at the Giant to this marriage today—for

her tenacity, and to you, Jimmy darling, for never being accused of making a hasty decision.' "

How, then, did he finally pop the question?

"I ran—"

"—out of excuses," Joni says, finishing Jim's sentence.

Joni Palmer, a photographer, also acts as *Jim Palmer*'s manager in his multilayered on- and off-camera career. They live in Baltimore, Maryland.

♥♥

Place: Hunter Mountain, New York
Setting: Ski Slope
Time: 1960

GLORIA and JACQUES PEPIN can often be found in the kitchen they designed and built from scratch in their Provençal house in Connecticut. A large room, encompassing a never-ending marble island, stoves, refrigerators, sinks, and an oak table large enough for a horde of gastronomes, this everything-in-its-place environment serves as metaphor for their relationship. Working together with ease, exchanging few words, they are always gracious hosts, feeding neighbors and notables alike. Gloria, with high cheekbones and close-cropped sandy hair, is a smaller version of Ingrid Bergman, while Jacques, with rosy cheeks and an impish grin, is a teddy bear, even without his toque.

"I was married when I met Jacques, who was teaching skiing, not cooking. My former husband, Dick Olmsted, and Jacques were on ski patrol at Hunter Mountain. Jacques was dating a friend of mine, but he said if I ever got divorced, I should call him. I did the next best thing," Gloria says. "I signed up for a private ski lesson." (Gloria adds that she may be the only woman, ever, to have divorced one Hunter Mountain Hall of Famer and married another.)

"Jacques was a very strict teacher. He would hit my legs with the ski pole and shout at me to bend my knees. As a result, I had to take two lessons before I could get to first base. After the second lesson he asked me to call him."

"A few days later, I called her," Jacques says.

"He was pretty nervy, but he was cute (he still is), so I agreed to have a drink with him after work in the city."

"I wanted to see her in a skirt instead of ski pants so I could check out her legs," he confesses with a blush.

"On our second date he cooked for me . . . a boeuf bourgignon and . . . it wasn't bad at all."

Jacques lived on Eighty-third Street and Gloria on Sixty-second. Every night, from the boeuf bourgignon on, he'd stop in on the way home.

"I was too intimidated to cook for him. So after work I'd rush home, cook something, and eat it in a hurry. Then, before he arrived, I'd walk the dog, stop at the corner deli, and buy cold cuts. I always used the same excuse: It's too late to cook.

"But one day I made the mistake of buying a thick slice of Virginia ham, and—just my luck—one of Jacques's favorite dishes was fried eggs and ham . . . could I cook them for him? I was trapped. I gingerly broke two eggs into the frying pan and said, 'Watch these, Jacques—I'll be right back.' I ran into the other room, hoping he would finish the job. When I peeked in, he was poking the yolks with a fork and sloshing them around in the pan. Then he slid the whole mess onto a plate with the ham and ate it with gusto. I wouldn't have touched the stuff—it looked awful—but from that moment on I knew I could cook for him. The guy would eat anything."

"We were married in 1966 on a bluff in East Hampton," Jacques says, "at Craig Claiborne's house."

"Jacques was in the kitchen—cooking, sweating—until twenty minutes before the ceremony. But this time, he had plenty of help . . . from Roger Fessageut, André Soltner, Craig Claiborne, Pierre Franey, Michel Keller, Jean Vergnes and Jean Claude Szurdak, who had worked for de Gaulle with Jacques, made the wedding cake. As usual, they were all trying to outdo one another."

However, even with too many cooks, this mixture never spoiled, only improved with age.

Jacques Pepin is an author and world-class chef. *Gloria Pepin,* once in the music business, often cooks with Jacques when not redesigning and rebuilding their new beach house in Connecticut.

Place: New York City
Setting: College Dorm, Columbia University
Time: March 1971

Anna Quindlen describes her first meeting with Jerry Krovatin in the same down-to-earth tone that characterizes her writing. She is quick and to the point, with little sentimentality and lots of heart, and her Irish-Italian heritage is instantly apparent. Because Anna looks younger than she is, it's hard to conceive of her as the weathered journalist with the world-in-your-backyard perspective, more widely read and quoted than many of her senior peers. But there she is—steel-trap mind encased in mom next door, her columns dog-eared and yellowing on refrigerators across America.

"Jerry and I met in the most pathetic Andy Hardy–movie fashion. We were both freshmen in college; I was at Barnard and he Columbia . . . and . . . we were both from New Jersey. There was a guy from Oregon on Jerry's dorm floor. As a matter of fact, he was probably the only guy from Oregon in the dorm," she says, laughing. "Anyway, he was ecstatic to find two people from the same state. Not understanding that half the people at Barnard and Columbia were from New Jersey, he insisted that Jerry and I meet."

That was at a tea in the living room of Anna's dormitory. It was March 3, 1971.

"Although I don't believe in love at first sight, it's too deep and complex an emotion," she says, "I can remember there was *something* at first sight on my part. All Jerry can remember is that I had on the shortest dress he'd ever seen in his life, which is true. I had made it myself, and basically, it qualified as a shirt."

Jerry asked Anna for a date that same day. She told him she had laundry to do.

"I'm not sure why I did that. The second time he asked, I accepted without hesitation. We went to see a Rolling Stones movie called *Sympathy for the Devil*," Anna says, rolling her eyes. "It had no plot line and was completely surreal. It was worse than seeing *La Strada*. I remember sitting there in the dark thinking, What if he understands this movie? I'm going to shoot myself."

As they left the theater, Jerry asked if she understood the film. "No, of course, I didn't," she said.

"Good. Neither did I," he replied.

That settled, they went to a nearby Baskin-Robbins for an ice-cream cone.

Anna remembers calling her mother to tell her that she had met "this guy," and her mother said matter-of-factly, "I thought you would." Anna, to this day a little incredulous, says, "She knew it even before I said it. She knew I meant *the* guy." However, her mother *was* "delighted" that he too was Catholic.

A certain ritual has developed over the years and is now an accepted part of Quindlen family folklore.

"I'm the oldest of five. My parents are two people who met, felt as if they had been hit over the head with a board, and got married. They were barely out of their teens. It's almost assumed in my family that when you're a teenager, you meet somebody, fall

in love, get married, and stay married for the rest of your life," Anna says. "It happened that way for most of my siblings, and it happened that way for me."

Although Jerry and Anna dated on and off for seven years before getting married, the romance that struck early stuck. And today, many years and three children later, they still live in New Jersey.

Anna Quindlen is a *New York Times* columnist and novelist. *Jerry Krovatin* is a criminal attorney.

♥ ♥

Place: Cambridge, Massachusetts
Setting: Snowy Bank of the Charles River
Time: February 1986

Though KYRA SEDGWICK and KEVIN BACON look young enough to be campus sweethearts, they're already settled down with two homes, a baby son, and a dog. Kyra's mix of wonder and worldliness—dark eyes dancing in a frame of blond curls—is a perfect counterpoint to Kevin's boy-next-door reserve.

"I had been really excited about working with Kevin. When I was a kid my mom used to see every piece of theater he was in and tell me this guy named Kevin Bacon was a really great actor.

"So the first time we met I was twelve, and Kevin was nineteen. My two brothers, Nikko and Robby, and I saw Kevin in a play called *Album*, and he was great. After the show we saw him going into a deli, and they convinced me to go in and tell him how good he was, which I did. Nikko thought I should remind

Kevin about it when I was cast in *Lemon Sky*. I figured he wouldn't remember but thought it would be great if he did. He didn't."

"At the last minute I agreed to do a film project for the *American Playhouse* series: Lanford Wilson's *Lemon Sky*," Kevin remembers. "I was just back from New Zealand ... barely had enough time to pack a bag and drive to Cambridge to start rehearsals at WGBH the next day. I had to stay at a different hotel from the rest of the cast because my dog, Jane, was with me."

The first day of rehearsals the studio van arrived filled with the cast, which included newcomer Kyra Sedgwick. Kevin and Jane climbed in.

"The minute I saw Kyra, I was smitten," Kevin says. "She was young, beautiful, and she had an incredible energy ... an unforced and graceful sexuality that was very exciting, though she did seem a little guarded about herself."

"Really? God, I always thought I opened my mouth too much," Kyra says.

"Not really. I had this fantasy about the life you led, your background. And your unavailability just made you more attractive."

"I was involved with someone else at the time, so I guess that's why I seemed standoffish. Actually I thought Kevin was stuck-up. He got into the van dressed in country chic—in a green wool Santa Fe jacket, country boots, jeans—with this dog, this black Lab. I thought, Okay, that's this guy's image, laid-back and cool. He barely looked at me; just said hi and looked away. I thought, God, that's totally rude.

"It's a very intense working experience when you're doing a play like this. During the first days of rehearsal you have to lay the

groundwork for what's going to be a very close series of relation-ships over the next couple of months. You have a lump in your throat at the first reading," says Kevin. "It's kind of like the first day of school."

As time passed, Kevin tried to organize things in the evening, going out for a drink or dinner with the cast, ever hopeful that Kyra would join them.

"Invariably," he says, "she'd go back to her room and do aerobics or something."

"The first few read-throughs, every time I'd look up from the script, he'd be staring at me and I thought, He thinks I'm bad. He thinks, I can't believe they hired this girl for the part, it's such a good part. I also thought he was involved with someone else. I mean, I never thought he was looking at me because he was *inter-ested*," Kyra says.

Kevin had been working out in the gym and getting massages at his hotel. When Kyra made an appointment for herself, he sug-gested that if they should happen to run into each other afterward, they could have dinner.

"Sure enough, after my massage he was there, showered, wait-ing. I thought, Wow, perfect timing."

"I had been trying to 'casually' bump into Kyra, and it never worked. This time I was going to get it right; that meant knowing if she was getting a half-hour or an hour massage. I couldn't ask her, so I tried to find out at the hotel by asking the price for a nonguest; then I had to see what price Kyra had been quoted. It was a logistical nightmare, but when she showed up, I acted as if I'd just gotten there. I had made dinner reservations in the hotel restaurant, which was nice but expensive."

"I opened up the menu and said, 'Oh, my God, what are we

doing here?' All the entrées were like thirty dollars," Kyra remembers.

"You were probably thinking I was acting like some rich movie star, trying to impress you," Kevin says.

"No, by that time I didn't. I really liked you."

Five minutes into dinner Kevin told Kyra he had just broken up with his girlfriend.

"We had a really, really great time that night," Kyra says. "I kept trying to convince myself that nothing was happening. I even called the guy I was seeing and said, "Look, you'd better visit me.' When he said he couldn't, I knew that was it. I allowed myself to fall madly in love."

"I was totally knocked out after that dinner. I wrote a song about her that night," Kevin says. "But I did feel a little apprehensive, as time went on, about pushing her into something. I didn't want her to break up with this other guy and then not have it work out. There we were, doing this play together, sneaking around snow-covered Cambridge . . . it was incredibly romantic. But working situations can be very unrealistic. It's easy for people to fall in love. It's kind of like camp. I've seen it happen a million times with leading men and women, and then afterwards, when they're back in their lives, they end up hating each other. You have to be really careful, and we talked about that a lot early on."

"I remember waking up every morning with a really warm feeling and thinking, It's Kevin, he's like home to me; he's like family. Of course, I was incredibly attracted to him, but it was deeper than that. I felt he would always be there, he would stick by me. I wasn't thinking of marriage or anything; there was just this beautiful feeling of total security and love. I had never felt that

before with anyone in my life, never, ever, with anyone. I feel as though we were meant to be together, in the heavens."

"Before I met Kyra, I had made up my mind to be alone because I had just broken up from a six-year relationship. The problem is, those kinds of decisions are intellectual, and love has nothing to do with the intellect. When you're shot in the heart, you can't take the arrow out."

Kyra Sedgwick and *Kevin Bacon* are actors who have worked in television, theater, and film. They live in New York and Connecticut.

Place: New York City
Setting: Simon & Schuster
Time: 1933

ANDREA SIMON—Andy to her friends—is an absolute replica of Katharine Hepburn: same hair, same trousers and work shirt, same bullet blue-eyed gaze, same love of nature, same ability to call a spade a shovel. The only difference is Andy's half Kate's size and has twice as large a family, her talented, now-grown children— Joanna, Lucy, Peter, and Carly—having produced an equally talented gaggle of grandchildren.

"Of all the things that happened to me in my life, the meeting with DICK SIMON was the most important," Andrea Simon says, adjusting a wisp from her graying topknot.

"I was working at Ditsons, the old music store on Thirty-fourth Street off Fifth Avenue, when I bumped into Jack Goodman, an old friend who was a staff editor at Simon and Schuster. He said, 'God, you look like hell, you should get off your feet. There's a job open at Simon and Schuster for a switchboard receptionist. Are you interested?' "

"I said, 'Oh, Jack, anything to sit down, anything!' So he

suggested I go over and see Mr. Shimkin, the manager, and have an interview.

"I didn't have a thing to wear, so I went to Altman's and stole a suit, which I returned after the interview. You see, I worked at Altman's once and knew about the rack reserved for salespeople, so I went to see my old friends and picked up a suit at the same time.

"During the course of my interview Mr. Shimkin asked if I was familiar with a switchboard, and I told him I had intimate knowledge of switchboards. Naturally I had never seen a switchboard up close before."

He told Andrea the job was hers, starting Monday, for eighteen dollars a week. It was 1933.

"Although it wasn't enough money, I accepted and learned how to operate the switchboard in about two minutes. Everyone passed by my desk, so I met lots of people that Monday: authors, staff, even Max Schuster. But no Richard Simon. When he finally stepped off the elevator, it was Thursday . . . but I knew exactly who it was.

"He strode right up to my desk and said, 'Good morning, little woman.' (Carly wrote a song about that, and there's a picture of Dick and me on that album.) So I said, 'Good morning, big man.' He was six feet five inches, you know. Right off the bat when I saw Dick, the minute I looked at him, the minute he said good morning, I knew that it was going to be *something* between Simon and me. And, God, was he handsome . . . devastatingly handsome, absolutely beautiful. What is it about those tall men?

"After that, when his girlfriends called, I would say, 'I'm terribly sorry, Mr. Simon's all tied up in conferences,' or, 'Mr. Simon hasn't come in yet. . . .' I often wondered if they asked why he never called back.

"During this time I occasionally had dinner with Neil, one of

our authors, who wrote *Farewell to Fifth Avenue* . . . Neil . . . Cornelius Vanderbilt, Jr. I think it was his only book. Anyway, Neil would pick me up in his chauffeured Duesenberg and take me to the Plaza or the Ritz, the Waldorf, or the Biltmore—anywhere one could have dinner and dance. He was a good dancer, Neil, attractive, too, but he wasn't my type. I was having a fine time, though. Eating—that was the main attraction. The first time I asked for a doggie bag I thought he'd drop under the table, he was so embarrassed. He said, 'I didn't know you had a dog.' I said, 'Oooh, yes, I have three dogs.' " ("My two brothers and my friend Ernest," she confesses now.)

"When Neil asked me to the Kentucky Derby, I went to Mr. Simon and asked if there was a company policy at Simon and Schuster about employees dating writers. He said, 'Why do you ask?' When I told him, his steel blue eyes flashed, and he said with considerable emphasis, 'As of now, *yes*, there is a policy!'

"After that, I couldn't get rid of him," she says, still triumphant. He was at the switchboard constantly: 'I'll take you to lunch, I'll do this, I'll do that.' Finally I conceded, and we went to Longchamps for dinner. He was delightful to be with, charming and fun, and I just loved to look at him. There were more dinners, lunches, concerts, and sometimes we would go to his apartment and perform duets. German lieder . . . I would sing and he would play. He was a beautiful pianist."

One summer evening, after a day at the beach, Richard drove Andrea to her apartment under the Ninth Avenue el in his Ford roadster with a rumble seat.

"He opened my door, put his hands around my waist, and lifted me onto the running board. Then he looked up at me—the first time he had ever looked *up* at me—and said, 'Let's get married.' My knees buckled.

. . . .

"I said, 'I think we'd better do a little talking.' He said, 'We have been talking.' So I threw my arms around his neck, kissed him, and we went back to his apartment and made love, for the first time, to a Debussy nocturne.

"The next day I went into Mr. Shimkin's office and said, 'Mr. Shimkin, you don't have to bother about that increase in salary.' (I never did get more than eighteen dollars a week.) 'You see, I no longer work for Simon and Schuster . . . just for Simon.' "

Andrea Simon is a mother, a grandmother, and a naturalist. *Richard Simon* was the cofounder of Simon & Schuster.

Place: New York City
Setting: Theater Audition
Time: 1946

ANNE JACKSON and ELI WALLACH are out of this world—a devoted, goofy, down-to-earth cooperative. You want to hang around, become a small part of their largess, figure out what makes them click. They listen. They interrupt. They banter. They surprise. And they laugh, loud and often, taking not much *too* seriously, including themselves. If you could bottle them, marriage counselors would be out of business.

"We're constantly asked, 'How do you make it work? What's the rule of thumb?' " says Eli. 'The answer is, we don't know."

"We fight a lot. Our kids still say, 'They're at it again.' But it's very hard to live with strong, stubborn personalities, which we both are. When I first met him, I thought Eli was tamed. Little did I know . . ." says Anne, her husky voice turning into a chuckle.

"Once we were on a television show where two women gave us a very effusive introduction: 'This marriage, this ideal, this couple'—gushing on and on. When we finally entered, dramatically, from archways on each side of the stage and met at the

microphone, Anne said, deadpan, 'What makes you think we're so happy?' "

"They had no idea how to handle that kind of humor . . . but you can't come on like goody two shoes."

From the conspiratorial laughter today, you know they had a great time that night.

"We're more fortunate than most actors in that we've been able to work together on and off over the years. There were sacrifices, and the sacrifices were usually mine; they had to be," Anne says. "With three children we could only travel one at a time. Occasionally it was me; more often it was Eli.

"From the beginning we were soul buddies . . . with a deep love for the theater. When we met, I think we were out to save the world, each with strong political beliefs, each terribly self-righteous. I respected Eli's sense of fairness as well as his radical ideas; those spirits were very strong in both of us."

That was in 1946, when they were cast in the Tennessee Williams's one-act *This Property is Condemned*, directed by Terry Hayden. Eli was fresh out of five years in the Army's Medical Corps; Anne was already an established ingenue.

"I auditioned in my uniform with all the 'fruit salad' (medals, ribbons, et cetera) and got the part. Anne had already been cast. She had long red hair and was quite—"

"—beautiful, say beautiful," Anne breaks in, and, along with Eli, cracks up. "Smitten, go ahead, say it. He was smitten with me."

"You were, and I was, but I was also in a relationship with a nurse overseas—"

"That's right. Both of us were spoken for."

"She was supposed to go to Alaska and live in a trailer with a poet—"

"My high school sweetheart; he wrote the most romantic Whitmanesque letters—

"I had just gotten back from a tour of *The Cherry Orchard* with Eva Le Gallienne, and I talked about it interminably . . . bored everybody stiff. But I think Eli was impressed with my stories, just as I was with his acting. He actually told me—I remember this; he doesn't—that he was a better actor than I was."

"George Hamilton once said, 'Women have computers for minds. They register everything,' " Eli says with a "gotcha" grin, "and call it up at the oddest times."

"We began dating and . . . romancing. In 1947 Eli had an audition for the American Repertory Theatre. . . ."

"We selected a scene from *Winterset*. I had all the lines; Anne said, 'Yes, Mio,' and 'No, Mio.' When we finished, they said thank you very much to me and offered Anne a two-year contract. I went off to Washington to do a Horton Foote play for five dollars a week."

"When he finished, there was an opening—it was fate—at the Rep. We spent the next year working together . . . five plays in one season on Broadway."

Fate seemed less compliant when Anne, almost cast in *Deep Are the Roots* in London, realized the liabilities for two working, traveling actors in one relationship. As it turned out, Betsy Drake took the part.

"She came back by ship, met Cary Grant on board, and married him. See, Annie, you could have married Cary Grant—"

"Oh, honey, never . . . never in a million years," she replies without a bit of irony.

After a year in *Antony and Cleopatra* with Katharine Cornell, Anne and Eli decided to get married.

"I brought her daisies," Eli recalls.

"Daffodils," corrects Anne.

Did he propose formally?

"No," he says.

"How did you get me then?"

"We got up one morning and got married."

"Is that right?" she says with a raised eyebrow. "I always said I married for talent, not money or looks—that's not true; I liked the way he looked. But Eli had a lot of preconceived notions about a wife—"

"She'd play tennis and swim," he says with a grin.

"I can't do either, I never went to college . . . but I *am* a Doctor of Fine Arts, I wrote a book . . . and I was very good on roller skates."

Still want to know what makes this relationship work?

"Who knows?" says one.

"It's like asking a centipede, 'Which foot do you start with?' " says the other.

With that, they're laughing. They're at it again.

Anne Jackson and *Eli Wallach* are actors. They live in New York City.

♥ ♥

Place: San Juan, Puerto Rico
Setting: A Party
Time: April 1956

WILLIAM (*Ironweed*) KENNEDY, aka Mr. Albany, could easily pass as
Mr. Dublin. Given the opportunity, the red-haired, ruddy-faced
author would make the ideal understudy for any one of his pugna-
cious characters, were it not for his gentle voice and soft manner. In
contrast, DANA KENNEDY's dark, vivacious good looks allow more
flexibility, on stage or off. And in real life she's been equally comfortable in both places.

Dana Segarra was an actress and dancer living in New York,
having just finished performing with the first national company of
Pajama Game, when she visited her family in San Juan over Christmas. It was 1956. Her sister Julie threw a party in her honor and
invited, among others, the associate editor of the Puerto Rico *World
Journal*, Bill Kennedy.

"I spotted Dana immediately—she was the most stunningly
beautiful girl I had ever seen—and managed to corral her in the

kitchen and monopolize her for the rest of the evening."

"I made him a sandwich," Dana says, smiling.

"She's still one of the great cooks of the century."

"Bill, it was a ham sandwich."

"I remember the first time you made dinner for me you served peas with onions . . . and that was way before Birds Eye thought of it."

Bill asked Dana to go out on New Year's Eve. She declined.

"She told me she had to stay home with her mother . . . a real put-down."

"I explained that it was a family tradition to be together at midnight."

"So I said, 'How about twelve-thirty?' "

"I said yes, and we stayed out until dawn," Dana says, "watching the sun rise over the ocean. It was very romantic, and . . . Bill was very good-looking."

"The next day we went to the beach, and I asked her to marry me. It happened . . . just like that. It was an overwhelming feeling—"

"—and a spectacular day."

But Dana didn't say yes right away. She left for New York on January 6 and told Bill she'd think it over.

"I wrote her a letter—a long letter—a prediction of what our life would be. . . ."

"I read that letter now, and it gives me chills; he had such self-confidence. . . ."

"I was just arrogant. I didn't know my ass from my elbow."

Dana replied by telegram. "It was instinct," she says. "I knew it was right. It read, 'Happy birthday. See you Thursday.'

"Bill called his mother in the States, who said, 'Wait a minute, let me get a pencil. He said, 'You don't need a pencil, I'm getting

married.' His mother was stunned. . . . I forget what she said. . . .' "

"What she said was, 'Is she Catholic?' "

"That's right, and my mother said, 'Why so soon?' to which Bill replied, 'Because I love her just as much today as I will a year from now.' "

Try . . . thirty-five.

Dana Kennedy is a former dancer and choreographer. *William Kennedy* is a novelist. They live in Albany.

♥♥

Place: Tokyo, Japan
Setting: Baseball Park
Time: 1978

"Diamonds are a girl's best friend" is *not* an anachronism when applied to NANCY LOPEZ, record-breaking Ladies Professional Golf Association champion and wife of baseball-diamond legend RAY KNIGHT.

"I always loved the Cincinnati Reds and thought Ray was the best third baseman there ever was," she says, dark eyes crinkling at the corners, Pepsodent smile widening. "When we found out they were in Tokyo the same week as our golf tournament, a group of us went to see them play. That was the first time I met him. In 1978."

At the time Ray was married and Nancy was engaged to a sportscaster who was transferred, a few months after their wedding, to Cincinnati, Ohio. Ironically, after an interview in the Reds' dugout, he and Ray Knight became good friends.

"Ray was one of the nicest people I had ever met. When my nephew Bernie was in town, he'd take him under his wing, introduce him to all the players. . . . Actually he became friendly with my entire family, always got them tickets when he played in California. He was incredibly kind."

Though Nancy, then in her early twenties, traveled a great deal for tournament play, she was disheartened when her husband was transferred again. This time to Houston.

"I also thought I'd never see Ray again," Nancy says, "and it made me sad. Not because I thought of him romantically but because he had become a friend. He was a gentle, good person . . . a nice man . . . and when you're on the road a lot, it's hard to develop friendships at home."

Four months later, as if by fate, Ray Knight was traded . . . from the Cincinnati Reds to the Houston Astros.

"It was like getting a friend back. I had begun to have problems in my marriage, and Ray was somebody that I could really talk to about it. He was very sensitive, he had been through it himself, he adored my husband, and he could see both sides. He encouraged me to stay and try to work it out."

Ultimately she was divorced but continued to see Ray, her closest ally.

"I had always thought Ray was gorgeous, with the prettiest blue eyes I'd ever seen—just because you're married doesn't mean you're blind—but I didn't think of him in terms of a 'relationship.'"

Nor did Ray.

"He thought I was too heavy. I was."

So she talked, he listened, but eventually lunches turned into dinners, albeit light ones; Nancy Lopez began to lose weight and . . . fall in love.

"That feeling was so wonderful. I simply adored him. We had always admired each other from afar, even before we met and became friends. I think, in the end, we both believe it was fated."

One night several months later Ray Knight proposed to Nancy Lopez. In his hot tub in Houston.

"He said, 'You wouldn't live with me, would you?' I said, 'No I wouldn't.' So he said, 'Well, will you marry me then?' "

After she said yes, Ray took Nancy home to meet his folks in Albany, Georgia, where they stayed a month. During that time Nancy learned to shoot a gun and eventually began to hunt with Ray, something they still do today on their six-hundred-acre farm in Georgia, to keep the freezer well stocked, year-round, for their growing family.

"We are extremely home-oriented people," Nancy says. "Each of us was raised that way, so we have a lot of love in our own family. It's our number one priority."

Theirs is an old-fashioned story . . . from fairway to fair play, with a graceful slide into home, for good measure.

Nancy Lopez is a golfer. *Ray Knight* has retired from baseball and is a sports commentator on ESPN. They live in Ray's hometown.

Place: New York City
Setting: The Ginger Man
Time: April 1978

The ice-blue eyes and the angel voice are unchanged, better maybe. But these days there's more: Rocky Mountain Productions, a fine-tuned autobiography, a novel on the way, more albums, sold-out concerts, a television special, and even a little time left over for painting. One might ask how anyone who lives with JUDY COLLINS puts up with that schedule.

"He's an artist, he's his own person, and he's as involved with his work as I am," says Judy, "plus we hit it off like gangbusters, right from the start."

That was on an April evening in 1978, when her friend Jean Livingston called to say she wanted Judy to meet "a darling guy" the following week at a party to benefit the Equal Rights Amendment (ERA) at The Ginger Man.

"Patrick [O'Neal] renamed his restaurant The Ginger Person for the event. There were ERA dinners all over town that night, and a bunch of us were committed to Patrick's: Bella Abzug, Gloria Steinem, Stephen Sondheim, Alan Alda, Jean Livingston, Bob Gerson, and Bob's partner ('a darling guy'), LOUIS NELSON.

"Louis was very attractive: great big blue eyes and a beautiful sparkling smile. (To this day he's much more photogenic than I am. I look like some mousy girl in the background; he looks . . . marvelous.) As we talked, a very aggressive man pushed a tape recorder in front of my face and played a song his kid had written. Louis ushered him away, making it very clear he wouldn't tolerate this hostile guy invading my privacy. That really impressed me."

In the three months that followed, Judy, as she says, "floated off into the ozone and rearranged my life." The biggest change, described candidly in her memoir *Trust Your Heart*, was conquering alcoholism. When Judy returned to earth, it was mid-July, and there was a call from Louis.

"He took me to his favorite restaurant, Orsini's. It had beautiful terra-cotta floors, high ceilings, ceramics on whitewashed walls, arched windows with lace curtains, and the best Italian food I've ever eaten. We talked and talked—and maybe I was just seeing things more clearly, but suddenly I realized how handsome he was—and talked. I think that's very rare—that feeling of having a lot to say to one another, of having a lot to say to anybody, for that matter. We talked until the restaurant was empty and the head-waiter was giving us dirty looks."

By August they were living together, and as Judy says, they haven't looked backward since.

"Sideways maybe," she says with a laugh. "I think we identify with each other and bring a similar eclecticism to our work, with certain basic ideas about art that we apply to different media. He's a wonderful artist, tops in his field. I can't imagine being with someone who isn't passionate about their work."

Judy admits that her touring is hard on the relationship but thinks that today any relationship when both partners work is difficult.

"It was a big help to start out with so many positives, though, and now I think we help each other. There's a synchronicity, even though we're total opposites. He's orderly, I'm sloppy; his process of arriving at a decision is very different from mine. But gradually we've begun to overlap: I've become a list maker, and he depends more on his instincts."

Judy Collins is synonymous with Colorado, so it's no surprise that after Orsini's came the Rockies and a rite of passage for Louis.

". . . an enormous family reunion . . . and Louis, climbing around in the mountains with all these people—something I'm sure he never thought he'd be doing. He instantly became part of the family."

Louis—a cross between a handsome sea captain and a Smith (cough drop) Brother with a sense of humor—comes from a small family with Norwegian roots.

"When Judy and I got to her mother's, this huge family piled out of this teeny house and surrounded me. Everybody, hugging and kissing; I don't even think there was an introduction. Her family was just the opposite of mine—going in a million directions at once, open, boisterous. I immediately felt very much a part of them. I guess," he adds with a grin, "I had no choice.

"Since then I've learned from Judy—and it's been good—that anything and everything can change at any time. I guess we've grown together . . . towards each other's polarities. . . . Sometimes it's terrible; sometimes it's wonderful," he says, breaking into that sparkling smile. "It's been a roller-coaster ride to heaven."

Judy Collins is a singer. *Louis Nelson* is an industrial designer. They live in New York and Connecticut.

♥♥

Place: New York City
Setting: Philco Television Playhouse Studio
Time: 1956

PEGGY and ARTHUR PENN are a study in contrasts. Quiet contrasts. Both are gentle, balanced, their serenity almost palpable—and no doubt welcome in their chaotic professions; he is a film director (*Little Big Man, The Miracle Worker, Bonnie and Clyde*), she a director of the Ackerman Institute for Family Therapy. Yet this calm ensemble exudes a lively curiosity . . . his like a leprechaun's, hers like a leopard's. Tranquil surfaces, spirited subtexts. No frills, no fanfare—no need.

In 1956 Peggy Maurer came to audition for a J. P. Miller play that Arthur Penn was directing for the Philco Television Playhouse.

"Peggy was an astonishing beauty," Arthur says with an elfin smile, blue eyes twinkling. "And a fine actress. I was extremely attracted to her, right off the bat."

Arthur offered to drive Peggy home after the audition. (She got the part.) This meant taking a cab down from the studio on Fiftieth Street to Eleventh Street, where his sporty little red Plymouth was parked. From there he drove Peggy to her apartment on the ex-

treme Upper West Side of Manhattan, proving that he was either crazy, smitten, or, perhaps, both: "crazy about Peggy."

At the time, she was starring in a highly acclaimed production of Chekhov's *The Three Sisters* at the Fourth Street Theater, one of the first New York theaters to emerge as an off-Broadway house. The show ran six nights a week, with back-to-back matinee and evening performances, four acts each, on Saturday and Sunday. That's why on her first big day of television rehearsals, Peggy Maurer overslept.

"I was mortified. I jumped into my jeans, flew out of my apartment into a cab, and arrived, completely apologetic, in a dither," Peggy says, her voice now, in contrast, a rich, deep, almost hypnotic contralto.

"She came in, contrite, looking as if she would be thrown out," Arthur remembers. "But I wasn't about to do that. I liked her too much."

"Arthur was adorable. He gave me his coffee, and kindly reassured me. Later, he took me to lunch, where he did all sorts of terribly funny imitations of actors and directors—he was just darling—and then asked me to have dinner with him that same evening. I accepted—it was Monday, the only night the theater was dark and I was free—but I literally had nothing to wear, save jeans and T-shirts."

Peggy put out a distress call to her two sisters (the Chekhovian siblings) and in short order they managed to come up with the perfect black dress.

"We went to the Charles restaurant, which was in the Village on Twelfth or Thirteenth Street. It was old and quite beautiful with wonderful food. However, Arthur, ordinarily smooth and self-assured, seemed rather nervous. I remember he spilled the wine and an entire dessert slid off his plate. But I also remember we did

a lot of sharing about Italian primitive painting, Europe, and the theater. We had so many things in common."

Arthur remembers having a spectacular evening. 'When I dropped her off, I kissed her and said something like 'Will you marry me?' . . . and I meant it, too. I had a terrific kind of click with Peggy. And it turned out to be the right time for both of us."

"I felt I should pull back a bit, which I did," says Peggy, "until about ten o'clock the next morning. It was so much fun working together. In the days of live television, the director stood right next to the actor, so I was playing all my love scenes with Arthur's face right next to mine. His directorial style was very quiet, very soft. Over the next few days, we told each other everything, about our families, our lives. By the end of the week, we had fallen in love."

They were married, eight months later, at Bill (*The Miracle Worker*) and Myra Gibson's house in the Berkshires.

"There were nine of us and we all walked down the 'aisle' together," says Peggy. "Then Arthur and I drove to Williamstown and took a room at the inn. We were wiped out. He was reading *Time*, I was reading *Newsweek*, and we both fell sound asleep."

How have they managed to stay together all these years?

"Problem-solving skills," says Peggy, suddenly thoughtful. "There were times when both of us thought it was perfectly awful, and then somehow, we'd manage to work it out. Either you do or you don't learn to solve marital problems together."

She pauses, then answers again, this time with a grin.

"Or luck. How's luck?"

Peggy Penn is a therapist and director at the Ackerman Institute of Family Therapy. *Arthur Penn* is a film director. They are the parents of two grown children and live in New York City and Massachusetts.

♥♥

Place: Los Angeles
Setting: Discotheque
Time: 1979

There was a time when BARBARA LAZAROFF, the storm-in-a-Wonderland-size-teacup restaurant designer, wanted to be a doctor.

"I was a Jewish girl from New York, studying medicine in Los Angeles, working hard and never going out," she says, readjusting a gargantuan fuchsia bow in her waist-length black hair with a perfectly manicured thumb and forefinger. "Just working, working, working.

"My friend Francesca was always after me to go to her club. She'd call and say, 'Come on, come on, go out, go out, go out.' Finally I said, 'Okay, okay, I'll go.'

"So we went to this discotheque and sat there watching everybody dance—" she says.

"With your halo on, right?" says WOLFGANG PUCK, world-famous and cute to boot Austrian inventor of American cuisine, taking a break from the grill at Eureka, their converted-brewery restaurant collaboration in West Hollywood.

"No, actually in those days I wore a flower in my hair. A real flower."

"And you had a dress slit up to here," he says, pointing to his hip.

"My birthday dress . . . do you remember the color?"

"Purple . . . no, burgundy, right?"

"Hey, I'm impressed. . . . Anyway, Wolf was sitting near me, but there was this fake painter between us—"

"He was a real painter," Wolf protests, laughing.

"A fake painter . . . he was a real *gigolo* who had decided to become a painter," Barbara continues. "Only his work looked exactly like everyone else's. This guy had too many lines, and I'm aggressive enough as it is. He kept bugging me, so I asked Wolf to dance."

After one dance (Barbara still complains about Wolf's stepping on her feet; he looks . . . sheepish) they sat and talked for the rest of the evening. She was a med student who liked to cook. He was a chef who liked to teach. He asked her to come to his cooking class the next day at Ma Maison.

"I thought she was a Beverly Hills type and probably wouldn't show up," Puck says.

"He was very good-looking and didn't speak enough English to insult me, so why not?" she replies.

However, the following day, she got lost en route to the restaurant and barely made the last five minutes of Wolfgang's class. "He was shy, keeping his eyes lowered as he talked," Barbara says, "but as he scooped a big wad of butter into his hand, he looked up, saw me standing in the back of the room, and dropped the butter— splat—on the floor."

"I blushed . . . turned bright red," Wolf says. "You see, the class was usually filled with little old ladies—"

"—who were always telling you how adorable you were, hugging you to their ample breasts."

Afterward he bought her an orange juice and tried to hold her hand.

"She kept pulling her hand away and told me she was involved with someone else. She said she just wanted to be friends. Be friends . . . sure, I'd heard that before."

"Even though I was dating someone else, I knew I was a goner," says Barbara.

A week later Wolf went to Europe, and Barbara took care of his Doberman, Bishop.

"The dog was psychotic. Wolf was never home—he's a workaholic—the dog was nuts, couldn't relate to human beings, so I'd visit Bishop every day, look into his eyes, massage his neck, and talk to him. I was rehabilitating him."

"And I was rehabilitating you," Wolf says, and they both laugh.

After *The Wolfgang Puck Cookbook* was launched and the Barbara Lazaroff design business was under way, after the opening of their restaurants (Spago and Chinois on Main in L.A. and Postrio in San Francisco) and after four years of a stormy relationship, Wolf finally said, "This is ridiculous. How are we going to get married if we don't get along better?"

"I remember we were in the bedroom," Barbara says, "and I leaned over, looked him straight in the eye, and said, 'This is *it*, buster; this *is* as good as it's gonna get.' "

"So I proposed to her . . . and we still don't get along."

They were married twice, once in L.A., where they spent their wedding night on the concrete floor of Chinois, which was to open the next day, and once again in the south of France.

"I spent a year preparing for the wedding in Les Baux," Bar-

bara says, hand-painting, printing, and rolling wedding invitations in three languages, arranging the horse-drawn carriages for the bridal party, the knights in shining armor, the chocolatiers and jugglers. "My gown was created by Zandra Rhodes, seven yards of printed chiffon cascading from a wimple, white on cream on white; everyone was in medieval costume. . . ."

"Peter Allen played the piano, the food was from L'Ousteau de Beaumanière [one of the few three-star Michelin-rated restaurants in the world, where Wolf apprenticed], and," he adds, sounding a bit weary, "the wedding lasted seventeen hours."

"All the townspeople thought we were royalty," Barbara says. "Little did they know I was just a girl from the Bronx who had always dreamed of a fairy-tale wedding."

Barbara Lazaroff is an interior designer. *Wolfgang Puck* is a chef. They live in Beverly Hills with their young son and an assortment of cats, parrots, and llamas.

♥♥

Place: New York City
Setting: Pocket Theater
Time: January 1969

BLYTHE DANNER and BRUCE PALTROW's story would be the stuff of good situation comedy were it not for their enduring twenty-two-year marriage. Still, there's potential. He's fast-talking, earthy, and very funny. She's understated, proper, and a little ethereal. He sports a ponytail; she, a moderate blond bob. He's a big-time producer-director for television; she's a big-time actress for stage and screen. But in spite of the overlay, theirs reads like a small-town romance.

In January 1969 Blythe Danner auditioned for an off-Broadway play about mixed marriages that Bruce Paltrow was producing.

"It was freezing, the dead of winter, snow and ice everywhere, and a windchill factor of zero. But it was the sixties, so all the actresses were wearing Saran wrap with no bras under their coats. All of them," Bruce says with a sly smile, "except Blythe. She came in wearing a huge coat, extra sweaters, big black galoshes, and this ugly brown old-lady suit."

"I was so proud of it," she says in mock protest. "It was a beautiful Saks Fifth Avenue suit—"

"Peck and Peck," he says, shaking his head. "Very Protestant."

"There I was, pouring my heart out onstage with Cleavon Little, when I hear a man making jokes, somewhere out in the dark beyond the footlights, about my attire. He was very funny—completely charming really—and I thought he'd be fun to know."

"We didn't start to date, though. We started to hang out. At Tibbs Coffee Shop, after Unemployment. She was two-fifteen; I was two forty-five. That's how we became pals. I didn't make a pass at her. It wasn't really appropriate because she was in the play, which, by the way, I hadn't yet raised the money for."

The show finally opened. When it closed, at the end of March, Blythe and Bruce had their first real date.

"Once we started to become romantic," Bruce recalls, "we were never apart again. We were completely committed, very quickly."

"Bruce is the most sane and honest man I've ever known. He loves women; women love him. I think it's his healthy balance of anima and animus. He cooks; he's been a nurturing father; he understands what women have to go through. When the kids were born, I was out working and Bruce was home with them, writing. I've always said he's my rock."

In the fall of '69 Blythe starred on Broadway in *Butterflies Are Free*. Opening night, Bruce says, he asked Blythe's father for her hand in marriage.

Makings of a sitcom. Take two.

"My mother planned the entire wedding," says Blythe. "Because I was in the play, I barely had time to buy my dress and arrive for the ceremony. She'd been given a list of who should sit

where at the reception, which she reversed, so for starters, all the divorced couples were seated together."

"Usually the bride's and groom's people sit on opposite sides of the church. In our case," Bruce says, "it was Jews on the right, Christians on the left. When the glass was broken, one side shouted, '*Mazel tov*,' and the other side practically jumped out of the pews."

They were married on December 14, 1969, in the oldest Episcopal church in the country, "bicultural pioneers."

Their secret?

Two words, Bruce says: "Okay, honey."

Blythe Danner is an actress. *Bruce Paltrow* is a producer. They live in Los Angeles and New York.

Place: Rome
Setting: Hotel Excelsior Bar
Time: 1953

From *Sophie's Choice* to *Darkness Visible,* WILLIAM STYRON has illuminated our lives by daring to speak the unspeakable. He's a large, ruggedly handsome man with wide, sad eyes that light up for a moment when ROSE—a poet, a guiding force behind Amnesty International, and his wife of nearly forty years—enters the room. Selecting his words carefully, a residual southern lilt barely discernible, he describes their first encounter.

"In the winter of 1952 I gave a talk to Louis Rubin's graduate writing class at Johns Hopkins. There were only about fifteen students in the seminar; Rose was one of them. We spoke briefly after the lecture, and though I remember her vividly as being a very beautiful girl, nothing happened. I shook her hand, went back home, and never saw her again."

Not until the fall of 1953, that is, when Styron was a fellow at the American Academy of Arts and Letters in Rome.

"There was a letter in my mailbox from a Rose Burgunder, telling me she was in town and, at Louis Rubin's suggestion, was

writing to see if we might get together. But I didn't connect the name with the girl I met in Baltimore."

"I was unfamiliar with Bill's work when he lectured in Maryland, but I couldn't believe he was a good writer. He didn't speak very well—he hemmed and hawed—and he was dressed badly," Rose says now, smiling and still very beautiful. "But he was attractive and seemed terribly sweet.

"A year and a half later I was living in Rome with a friend from Wellesley, writing a book of poetry that I had a nice contract for and dating a very dull classicist from the academy. One day, passing the mailboxes there, I noticed Bill's name and scribbled him a note."

Bill called Rose and suggested they meet at the Hotel Excelsior bar for a drink. What he didn't tell her was that two other fellows would be in tow: a sculptor named Stephen Green and a writer named Truman Capote.

A week later, when Rose arrived at the Excelsior, Bill's table was a bit more crowded than she'd expected.

"It was obvious Bill was taking no chances. He was flanked by two other guys: one a sculptor, and the other a small, funny fellow in a sailor suit. It was a terrific evening, with lots of talk, energy, and laughter. After that Bill and I began to date—spent an entire month walking from one end of Rome to the other. That's how we got to know each other; we loved to walk together. . . . We still do."

Bill's friends from the academy became Rose's, and soon they took a small apartment together next door.

"From the very beginning we were madly in love with each other." Rose pauses and smiles. "It was really a hot romance . . . from late October to December."

At Bill's suggestion they decided to spend Christmas in Paris,

where he had lived and helped start *The Paris Review* the year before.

"He wanted me to meet all his friends—Peter Matthiessen, George Plimpton, John Marquand, and Tom Guinzburg. The night before we left, Bill proposed to me at the Flora Bar, two hotels up from the Excelsior, at the top of the Via Veneto."

On May 4 the Paris crew did a reverse commute, to Bill and Rose's wedding at Irwin Shaw's house outside Rome and afterwards to a nearby restaurant where they danced under a grape arbor until dawn.

Their postwedding holiday in Ravello ended up lasting a year. He was working on a novel, and she, a book of poetry. Neither was published, testament perhaps to the liveliest and longest literary honeymoon on record.

Rose Styron is a poet and a director of Amnesty International. *William Styron* is a writer. They live in Connecticut.

♥ ♥

Place: Paris
Setting: An Apartment on the Left Bank
Time: 1961

In a recent gala exhibition called "Broadway!" there were posters and playbills extolling HAL PRINCE'S extraordinary contributions to the American musical theater. His shows—*Damn Yankees, Pajama Game, West Side Story, Fiddler on the Roof, A Funny Thing Happened on the Way to the Forum,* to name a handful of early hits—are also in evidence on all four memorabilia-crammed walls of his office, a bustling enclave a long stone's throw from Shubert Alley.

It's been said that in later collaborations with Stephen Sondheim (*Company* and *A Little Night Music*) Hal Prince "turned a light on the many faces of marital relationships." That light, irrepressible, beneath trademark tortoiseshells propped on a shiny, fringed dome, intensifies when he speaks of his marriage to JUDY, his wife of thirty years.

"She's private. I'm public. I'll talk. She won't. She's much more musical than I. She's a concert pianist and a brilliant dancer; she's a terrific mother, she's beautiful, and she has the best brain of anyone I know—quite simply, one of the smartest people I've ever met."

The only way to follow that act is to start again, at the beginning: the summer of 1960. Hal Prince was on holiday, the first in six, hit musical years, visiting some American friends, George and Ethel Tyne, in Paris. Ethel's nineteen-year-old daughter, Judith Chaplin, was at their apartment the same evening.

"I asked her to join us for dinner at a wonderful restaurant, the Novy, which was White Russian and very dramatic, with red damask tablecloths, candlelight, champagne in silver buckets, violins, and gypsy singers. The conversation was swift and fun. Judy was very bright, very attractive," Hal says with a twinkling eye, "and we discovered that we had met once before, at her father's [Saul Chaplin, a composer from the golden days of MGM musicals] house in Hollywood when she was fourteen and I was a fledgling producer-writer working on a screenplay for *Pajama Game*."

That fall, after modeling for Nina Ricci and doing small parts in feature films, Judy came to New York and, making the overture, called Hal.

"We went to a lot of glamorous places in those days—El Morocco, Billie Reed's Little Club, the Stork Club—and stayed out very late, something," Hal says with a laugh, "we haven't done since.

"Judy joined her family in the spring of '61 in Pisa, and I flew over later and met them in the south of France. Both her parents, Ethel and Saul, were there, and though remarried, they were all good friends."

Hal remembers spending a day—name-dropping time, he says—with Ellen Barry, Philip Barry's widow, and Scottie Fitzgerald, Scott and Zelda's daughter, cruising the Riviera coast in a launch.

"It was one of those perfectly clear, sparkling days. We dropped anchor, swam, had lunch, and spent the rest of the after-

noon listening to stories from the perspective of two generations."

Ellen pointed out the houses on the hill where Philip Barry wrote *Hotel Universe* and where Isadora Duncan, shortly after Scottie had been put to bed, flung her scarf 'round her neck and sped off to her death.

That fall they returned to New York, and slowly Hal began to gather the courage to propose.

One of his and Judy's favorite haunts, but certainly not the toniest ("a pretty sleazy place," Hal says), was a little bar on Madison Avenue in the Sixties, where Hal finally popped the question, in a roundabout way.

"I hemmed and hawed and said something like 'If I were to ask you to marry me, what would you say?' And she said, 'I'd say yes.' Delighted, I called the waiter over and said, 'This girl has just accepted my marriage proposal; we'll have a bottle of your best champagne.' He gave me this 'sure, buddy, sure' look, probably thinking he'd just heard the fastest line in town.

"Since then it's only gotten better. I don't want to sound gooey," Hal says, "it's been hard work . . . but it's also been a very good life. Who would change it?"

Judy Prince is a musician and perhaps the most revered wife in America. *Hal Prince* is a producer and director.

Place: New York City
Setting: Pharmacy/Restaurant
Time: The 1980s

When BRENDA KING and ROY SCHEIDER smile in tandem, their sun-filled apartment seems to light up an extra notch. A handsome pair they appear to be, even before speaking in perfect sync.

Brenda, a tall, slender blonde with natural warmth and openness, remembers her early days in Manhattan without a trace of nostalgia.

"I was working as a model and an actress," Brenda says. "Ann Reinking, my roommate, had returned to New York after touring with *1776* [where the two met originally, through their respective actor husbands] and had been cast in *Pippin*. We were great friends . . . still are."

They shared an apartment in Manhattan's West Seventies (just down the block from where Brenda lives today, twenty years later), having met in the throes of their earlier too-young, short-lived marriages. Identical Sears sewing machines, purchased together, were the only domestic remnants of their first unions.

"When Annie was working on *All That Jazz,* I never made it to the studio in Ansonia to watch rehearsals," Brenda says. "But one

day, right after the film was released, I saw Roy Scheider, Ann's costar, in Zitomer's, an East Side pharmacy."

Brenda approached Roy, introduced herself as an actress, as an admirer of his work, and as Ann Reinking's roommate. He thanked her, asked about Annie, chatted briefly, and went on his way. The first connection.

The next time they saw each other was at the Beverly Hills Hotel. "I was living in Los Angeles by then and meeting a friend from out of town," Brenda remembers. "Roy was by the pool, getting too much sun, as usual."

They nodded hello and waved from afar. The second connection.

Then, in 1982, Brenda returned to New York City with her friend Shirley MacLaine. The night after they arrived, there was a gala Christmas dinner at Tavern on the Green, where Brenda met lots of Shirley's old friends, including a writer named Noel Behn. Coincidentally, three nights later, Shirley and Brenda bumped into him at Elaine's, the renowned "stars-at-the-front-table" watering hole on First Avenue. He was sitting with Roy Scheider. The third, and perhaps charmed, connection.

"Brenda, hi, come on over. There's someone I'd like you to meet." As Noel began to introduce them, Brenda interrupted. "Oh I know Roy. I've had a crush on him for years." ("Being a real smartass," she says now.)

Roy followed up quickly with "Of course, I know Brenda . . . and the crush is mutual."

"Does this mean we're engaged, Roy?" Brenda quipped.

"Brenda," Roy said, looking her straight in the eye, "you keep forgetting. We've been married for years."

Brenda "turned bright red" and beat a hasty retreat.

"It was very odd," she says, "like a karmic moment . . . a little

spooky, very strange. In one way it scared the hell out of me. I started out being flip, and then I was leveled."

Roy, however, was married at the time and going through a very difficult period. For a year and a half he and Brenda had an on-again-off-again relationship before Roy returned to his wife, determined to make the marriage work. Ultimately it did not. After three years of absolutely no contact, Roy called Brenda to explain his bizarre behavior. The moment they saw each other, Roy realized he was still in love with Brenda. Six months later they were married.

"We both believe it was fated. And I think you have to pay attention to those signposts and honor the moments. It's the synchronicity of life," Brenda says, and adds with a grin, "Anyway, when you're a friend of Shirley MacLaine's, what else could you expect?"

Brenda King is a painter and documentary filmmaker. *Roy Scheider* is an actor. They live in New York City and on Long Island with their son, Christian.

♥♥

Place: Hyde Park, New York
Setting: Elliott Roosevelt's House Party
Time: The 1930s

JANE WYATT is best remembered as the quintessential fifties mom on *Father Knows Best*. Today her spacious Beverly Hills living room, gardens visible from every window, has the same comfortable quality as her instantly recognizable voice. Yet when she and her husband, EDDIE WARD, begin to describe their courtship, the milieu seems as remote as the utopian valley in *Lost Horizon,* the 1937 Frank Capra classic in which Jane starred.

"I was in my first year at Harvard," Eddie remembers. "My friend and classmate Jimmy Roosevelt asked me to come to Hyde Park for New Year's Eve. . . . He and Elliott were having a few friends for the weekend. After visiting with relatives in New York, I got on the train at Grand Central, which was practically empty, except for two young, and very attractive, girls."

"My friend Leila Delano, the Roosevelts' cousin, and I were dressed to kill that day," Jane says, "high heels and everything. We were to be Elliott Roosevelt's guests at Hyde Park. The boys were all at Harvard, but Leila and I were only juniors at the Brearley and Chapin schools for girls. As we walked down the aisle, we

spotted Eddie but, of course, pretended we didn't. We just coyly sat down across from him. Eventually we discovered we were all going to the same place. It was terribly exciting, talking to an older man. Neither of us knew any college freshmen."

"Jane was having a problem tying her shoe—"

"My high heels had lacings—"

"So I tied her shoe, showed her how to make a knot that would never come undone. Wasn't that chivalrous?" Eddie says. (Not to mention symbolic.)

"A few months later I went to a dance at Groton with Elliott, and Eddie was there, but he had to stay up in the balcony. You had to be a Groton alumnus to dance, so I went up and talked to him for most of the evening. He was divine. Later we snuck downstairs to dance, something Eddie did beautifully. Dancing was a big part of our life in those days: tea dances, deb parties. It was wonderful exercise actually.

"In the intervening years I saw Eddie on and off . . . between his travels and tennis around the world. His mother had a place in Florence, which was a temporary home base, but when he was in New York, he always called. He was so Continental . . . glamorous, really . . . and a beautiful athlete.

"I was doing a Philip Barry play, *The Joyous Season*, when Eddie breezed into town," Jane recalls. "He took me to '21' after the show, for what I'm sure he thought would be a light supper. But I was ravenous and ordered a full-course dinner. He still laughs today about my appetite that night."

"I had a skiing accident in Switzerland a few months later," Eddie says. "My leg was badly broken, and it became so infected (this was before antibiotics) that I almost lost it. When I was finally well enough to travel, I was flown to Los Angeles to recuperate at the Good Samaritan Hospital for three months."

"The very same three months I had come to L.A. to be in the movies. When I got to my hotel, I called him immediately and said, breathlessly, 'Guess who this is?' and he said, 'I make it a policy never to guess over the telephone.'

"So I began to visit him—in person—every day. We'd often have dinner at the hospital, where, believe it or not, the food was wonderful: filet mignon, lobster tails, vanilla bean ice cream. . . ."

After Eddie was released, he finished mending at a house his mother owned in Santa Barbara. There was an enormous palm tree in the backyard that Jane decided to climb one afternoon.

"I got about halfway up, show-off that I was, and then fell out and dislocated my knee. Now *I* was the one laid up on the couch.

"The next day, although he was still on crutches, Eddie managed to get down on his knee and propose. And I didn't have to think too long before I said yes."

Jane Wyatt is an actress. *Eddie Ward* is a retired professional tennis player and businessman.

♥ ♥

Place: University of Georgia
Setting: Locker Room
Time: 1980

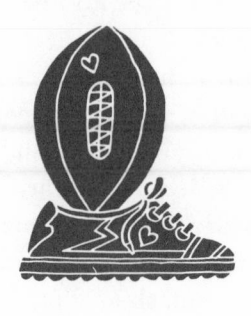

From the start CINDY and HERSCHEL WALKER were on the right track. That was in 1980, when she was a sophomore, he was a freshman, and both were on scholarships at the University of Georgia. Cindy, a middle-distance runner, got to know Herschel's sister Veronica, a track teammate. Herschel, a sprinter and soon-to-be-star fullback for the Georgia Bulldogs, was the number one high school recruit in the country that year.

"I hung around the girls' track team because Veronica was my friend, my family—we were close, seven kids, growing up in the Georgia countryside with no one but each other to play with—and I didn't go out with girls. Never dated, never drank, never smoked. I guess some people thought I was geeky," the soft-spoken six-footer confesses, "but I think I was self-confident. I didn't have to follow the crowd."

To judge from his still-rock solid frame, probably no one was in a rush to push him either. No one except Cindy DeAngelis, a compact, pretty brunette with Italian roots and moxie to spare.

"He fell in love with me right away, but I kind of blew him off," she says, laughing.

"I don't think that's right—"

"—then you must have lied to me. . . ."

"We met in the whirlpool," Herschel says.

"I was in the whirlpool; you were in the ice," Cindy specifies.

"That's right. But she didn't pay any attention to me—"

"I did, too. I answered your questions, which were all about sports—"

"—then we went out a couple of times, and she fell in love with me."

Now they're both laughing.

"No, we were just friends. We didn't date the first year. It was the second year when I decided to like him. Actually the summer in between is when it hit me, came upon me one day, out of the blue, just like that. I knew I was going to marry him."

"That was the farthest thing from my mind," says Herschel. "I didn't think I'd get married until I was in my thirties."

But Herschel's legendary success on the college gridiron led to a lucrative bid from the New Jersey Generals, and in his junior year he decided to move north and begin a career in professional football.

"It was a little scary. I don't think I could have done it without Cindy."

"But I said, 'I won't keep living with you. Make me an honest woman, or I'm out of here.' (You have to do that with men; they get cold feet.)"

They were married two days later, on March 31, 1983, in a small civil ceremony in Bloomfield, New Jersey.

"We've always enjoyed each other, we enjoy life, we still do just about everything together—"

"—including running," she adds, smiling, "every day."

In describing Herschel, Cindy says he's generous, funny, gentle and weighs in at 222.

"Two eighteen," he says quickly.

"I knew you'd say that."

Herschel says, "Cindy is five feet three inches—"

"Five feet four inches," she interrupts.

"Five feet three and a half inches . . . and very tough with a good heart," he says. "People think that when you marry young, you won't make it, but that's just talk. Our philosophy is, if people got paid for talking, everyone would be rich."

Cindy Walker is a cook and a runner. After playing with the Dallas Cowboys, *Herschel Walker* joined the Minnesota Vikings. They live in Dallas with their Rottweiler, Al Capone.

♥♥

Place: New York City
Setting: Mount Sinai Hospital
Time: January 1982

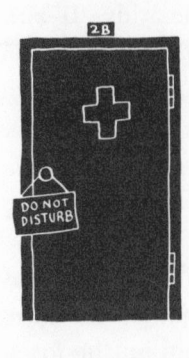

VALERIE HUMPHRIES is tall, slender, and capable, with size-you-up-in-seconds blue eyes, the kind of person who won't take guff from anyone, including JOSEPH HELLER, the best-selling (*Catch-22, Good as Gold, Something Happened*) novelist and occasional self-confessed curmudgeon.

It's a straightforward story. A patient falls for his nurse. Unable to move from the neck down, paralyzed by Guillain-Barré syndrome, a rare disorder that attacks the nervous system, the victim is active one day, immobilized the next. But when a woman with a combination of great bedside manner, gab, and good looks comes on the scene, there is, if you'll excuse the expression, a catch.

"I expected him to look like Norman Mailer. I expected wrong," Valerie says. "When I first saw Joe in his hospital bed at Mount Sinai, he was very frail, with lots of white hair and the

remnants of a tan. He was almost completely paralyzed, but he still talked a blue streak."

"I could move my head and bend my arms very slightly," Joe says now, fully recovered, miraculously vigorous, looking younger than his years.

"And smile," Valerie adds. "I knew I had to keep a conversation going. He was so much fun that I began looking forward to going to work. I even started to wear makeup."

"And she was quite taken by my visitors: Mario (*The Godfather*) Puzo, Mel (*The 2000-Year-Old Man*) Brooks, Dustin (*Little Big Man*) Hoffman, Arthur (*New York Times*) Gelb, Joe (*Fiddler on the Roof*) Stein—"

"They were loyal but kept their physical distance. . . . I think they were afraid of giving him something. So on the fourth day, as I was leaving, I kissed him on the forehead."

"Valerie and I became very friendly very quickly. At the beginning of the third week I knew she'd move downtown to Rusk with me for my rehabilitation."

"I wanted to stay . . . because I liked him, because it was a good steady job—"

"—and because Rusk was a lot closer to your apartment!" Joe says.

"I didn't want anybody taking over my territory!"

"I think she worked for me fifty-two days straight, without time off."

Gradually, as chronicled in *No Laughing Matter*, the book he coauthored with Speed Vogel, Joseph Heller began to improve. Regaining the use of his arms, he could now extend them to give Valerie a hug or pick up the phone and call her after hours.

"Back home, before going to bed, I'd turn off the phone and

turn on the answering machine. When I woke up, the first thing I'd hear was Joe's recorded voice—"

"I was awake by five every morning, so I'd call and leave the weather report, baroque music—"

"—and some very erotic messages. On those days," Valerie says, smiling, "I couldn't get to work fast enough."

"Belle Simon, Paul Simon's mother, stopped in every day because her husband's room was across the hall from Joe's. Once she caught me giving Joe a big kiss, came in, sat down, threw up her hands, and said, 'Oh, God, they're at it again.' "

"When I was discharged in the spring, I had to negotiate with Valerie to come to East Hampton for the summer. I was in a wheelchair by then and—"

"—it was the best job I ever had," she says. "Joe had a beautiful house near the beach, a pool, a garden—"

"—she was still getting paid . . . and eventually, I was able to climb the stairs." (Valerie's bedroom was on the second floor.)

From the beginning Joe had to rely on conversation, on his ability to make her laugh—like any courtship, he says—and on his friends, who took her to the theater and ballet.

"I arranged for the tickets, so she couldn't leave town for the weekend. The one weekend she did go away, she got the flu. Served her right."

"I knew from the beginning that we'd end up together. It happened just at the right time, for both of us. As a matter of fact, during most of his illness I was walking on air," she says, laughing along with Joe.

"I often told Speed that in many ways the Guillain-Barré changed my life . . . for the better."

Was their meeting fated? Heller responds in an instant.

"Yes. I think it was," and he adds, with a twinkling eye, "Joe Stein's wife's mother thought so too. She said we were a *shiddach*. That's Yiddish for a 'match made in heaven.'"

Valerie Heller is a retired nurse. *Joseph Heller* is a writer. They now share the same second-floor bedroom in their house in East Hampton.

♥♥

Place: Charlottesville, Virginia
Setting: University of Virginia
Time: 1985

It's easier to title the ANN BEATTIE and LINCOLN PERRY story than it is to follow it. "The Endless Hello" or "Too Many Good-Byes" might best sum up a circuitous route to the altar or, in their case, front porch.

It began in 1985 when Lincoln Perry moved to Charlottesville to teach for one semester at the University of Virginia. An artist—primarily a painter—living in a fifth-floor walk-up on New York's Lower East Side and struggling with a tempestuous at best relationship, Lincoln was no doubt relieved to have a break from emotional as well as urban upheaval.

"A friend told me I should look up Ann Beattie. I wasn't familiar with her work, so I went to the library, took out *Distortions* [her first], and called her after I'd read it."

Lincoln found her number in a tattered Charlottesville phone book pulled from a shelf in his temporary office and, as it turns out, the *only* phone book in which Ann Beattie had been listed . . . mistakenly.

"It was a 1983 directory," he says, "and though she had re-

quested an unpublished number, there she was. If she hadn't been listed, I never would have called."

Lincoln Perry was not the tracking-down type. And because he wasn't the asking-out type either, their first meeting was at Ann's house.

"When he called, there were so many pauses that I finally had to ask him over for a cup of coffee," Ann says, adding, as a postscript, "Charlottesville manners."

"When she opened the door, she was surrounded by light from the hallway behind her. Actually I remember her being backlit—as if she had an aura—the entire time I was there."

Ann remembers two things: "He had the most beautiful blue eyes imaginable, and he was terribly overwrought."

From this point Lincoln's on-again-off-again New York relationship cast a shadow of ambiguity—back, front, and center—on this newly formed alliance. But humor saved them—at least in retrospect. Hers is constant, ironic, fast-paced. His is self-deprecating, droll, deliberate. Both are masters at run-on dialogue.

At the end of their first meeting ("funny atrocity stories about college and postcollege lives," though Lincoln remembers Ann saying it's not *what* is said, but *how* it's said; the *tone* is what matters) Lincoln's departing words suggested a wish for reunion: "I hear you're a great cook."

"Well, er, I'm, uh, terrible at issuing invitations," Ann replied, nonplussed, "but you could phone sometime and invite yourself, I s'pose."

Lincoln called the next morning and was seated in Ann's dining room Saturday evening, with her friends Del and Larry.

"They talked, I cooked," she recalls, "slavishly, bringing out course after course. When Del and Larry left, Lincoln, who drinks

very little, asked if I had any brandy. I gave it to him, he poured himself a very generous glass, took a sip, and asked—"

"I had to steel myself to say it," Lincoln interrupts. "I said, 'Would it be obnoxious of me to ask to spend the night?' "

"It was unclear whether he wanted to sleep with me," Ann says, "or on the sofa—by this time I couldn't predict this person at all—so I started taking my clothes off on the way up the stairs."

Lincoln followed ("I had no intention of sleeping on the sofa") and the next morning spontaneously picked up the phone and improvised a scene, pretending to be Ann's lawyer, using his best Big Daddy drawl (Lincoln can imitate *any* dialect, flawlessly) to expedite a furniture delivery. As he was leaving, the armoire arrived and Ann was impressed.

"It was great. He was one of the oddest men I'd ever met. People are drawn to him like a magnet. His nickname is Charmball."

But after half a dozen "dates," Charmball packed up and headed back to New York and the "other woman."

"He left me. He left me," Ann repeats in mock accusation as Lincoln does a real squirm in his chair.

"Then he came back to Charlottesville for two days at Christmas. He gave me a watercolor he had painted. I gave him a key to the house."

"But it was wrapped up, and I didn't open it until I was back in my rat-infested walk-up," Lincoln adds, for drama. "Then I was really miserable. Completely depressed. Very confused."

"No . . . he was just a nice stable person," Ann says, "acting like a lunatic. He would say to me, point-blank, that he didn't know what he was doing with his life. He even had the nerve to ask me if I got frustrated with all my depressed characters, suggesting I might be happier with a larger palette, a more diverse group of

characters, like Shakespeare's. Here's this man who can't make up his mind, this man who has never taken me on an official date, wanting me to be Shakespeare!"

Now Lincoln's laughing helplessly as Ann manages to hold steadfast her supercilious gaze.

"On the other hand," she continues, "when his show opened in a local gallery, I was expecting an upbeat series of paintings—he'd previously characterized his work as Hallmark-card-cheerful—and found dark, harsh, grim stuff—"

"Now wait a minute . . ." Lincoln interrupts, laughing along with Ann.

As Lincoln boomeranged on the New York–Charlottesville axis, Ann became increasingly frustrated. After endless phone hours, many sit-down talks, and a stand-up on New Year's Eve, Ann Beattie, disgusted, decided she was absolutely, unequivocally finished with Lincoln Perry.

That is, until he called Ann's answering machine (in Charlottesville) to find she was staying with friends (Stephani and Robert) in New York and called their answering machine to leave three imploring messages that boiled down to "I can't live without you." This was followed by a series of calls from a wary Ann in midtown phone booths (between appointments), who finally agreed to meet an eager Lincoln downtown at One Fifth (the restaurant), where he apologized, admired her beauty, explained, and cajoled until she finally relented, forgot (sort of), and forgave. Then they went uptown to the Algonquin to meet Stephani and Robert, who were so suspicious of Lincoln that they had formed a human chain that morning to prevent her from seeing him but who ended up liking him, after all, because he was charming, funny, and contrite (gorgeous, too, Stephani confided to Ann in the ladies' room). Finally Lincoln and Ann went crosstown to the UN Plaza Hotel because

the Algonquin was full, and when they got to their room, Lincoln, who was exhausted, went to sleep and Ann, who was starved, ordered a sandwich.

Night fell.

The next morning they rented a car, drove to Maine, visited friends, drove back to New York for Lincoln's second (and final) therapist's appointment (the doctor said Lincoln seemed changed, better, fine really), Ann drove to Zabar's, bought sandwiches, returned to pick up Lincoln and suggest they drive to Charlottesville in the snow, which they did after he canceled his dentist appointment and packed up a grocery bag of paints and brushes from his apartment, where he never lived again because he finally proposed to Ann on his birthday, and even though she didn't believe him at first, they were married in blue jeans the following summer. On a front porch in Maine. With three people in attendance.

There were loads of other details, but this is the gist of it. And without a doubt, it's most probably, almost positively, exponentially safe to stake anything on this team. They're in it for the long run. And then some.

Ann Beattie is a writer. *Lincoln Perry* is a painter. They live in Maine and Virginia, never New York.

♥ ♥

Place: Los Angeles
Setting: Columbia Pictures Studios
Time: The 1950s

In the fifties sound stages were supposed to be soundproof. JACK LEMMON, some forty years later, with that irresistible *mea culpa* grin, heartily refutes the claim. His evidence dates back to the days he was under nonexclusive contract at Columbia Pictures.

"Bombs could have gone off when I was shooting, and generally I wouldn't have been thrown. But one day, in the middle of a take, for I can't remember what picture, I was aware of someone roaring with laughter. It was coming through the soundproof wall of the stage next to ours," Jack Lemmon says, still amazed.

"It was a woman's laugh, and I thought, Whoever the hell that is, I've got to meet that person. So I went next door, and there was this absolutely gorgeous girl, FELICIA FARR," Jack says. "And by the way, to this day that laugh still gets me."

They both were under contract at Columbia, but Jack, who was married at the time, says, "It wasn't one of those hidden things, where I was dying or pining away for her. It was the laugh."

Dorothy Blair, head of the studio's promotion department,

called Jack and his wife, Cynthia, a few months later to set up a routine studio publicity shot.

"We were living in West Los Angeles, and Dorothy had arranged for some movie magazine to do a piece on us having a casual backyard barbecue, entertaining Felicia Farr and her 'arranged' date, Cliff Robertson, an old pal of mine," Jack says.

Cliff and Jack had been waiters and part-time performers at the Old Nick in New York for "five bucks a week and a free meal every night—chicken in a basket." Jack also was the 143-pound bouncer.

"Needless to say, I never threw anybody out," he says, with a grin, and adds, "Maureen Stapleton, Jack Albertson . . . all kinds of people, mostly struggling actors, went through that place. . . . We had a lot of laughs.

"Anyway, the four of us did the barbecue shots," he says, "but for some reason it was never printed. Cynthia and I were divorced about a year later, and after working for a couple months overseas on *Fire down Below*, I came back to Hollywood and was, for the first time in a long time, on my own."

A good friend of Jack's, Freddy Karger, a musician and songwriter, also in the music department at Columbia, suggested that they go down to Studio 8 one evening before going to Dominic's, their favorite "joint" near the studio.

"He wanted me to meet this beautiful actress he hoped would join us for dinner. Felicia Farr. Did I know her?"

When they got to the studio, Jack spotted Felicia sitting on a wardrobe trunk on a western set in a floor-length dress with old-fashioned high-button shoes.

Though Jack's memory of the moment is clear, he's still starry-eyed as he tells it. "She looked up, smiled, and I . . . *went* . . . just like that. I was gone. After that I have no idea what we said. I was

in a bloody daze. I guess I hadn't allowed myself those feelings before."

The three of them arranged to have dinner a few nights later, but at the last minute Felicia canceled. Jack remembers being a little reticent about asking her for a "real" date, having not had one in many years. And Felicia, who was also divorced, wanted to get home to her small daughter, Denise, after work each day. Finally she agreed to go to a charity benefit with Freddy . . . and Jack.

"Luckily for me and unfortunately for Freddy, his band was playing, and he asked me if I would stand in for him," Jack says, with a raised eyebrow. " 'Sure, I'd be glad to help out . . . anything, for a pal,' I told him, 'anything.' "

Jack danced with Felicia "every moment he could, as close as possible and as far away from Freddy's band as he could get."

At the end of the evening there was a prolonged discussion about who would take Felicia home.

"No sooner did we get in the door of her house," the victor recalls, "than the phone rang. It was Freddy, making sure Felicia was home, safe and sound."

In the end Freddy took defeat gracefully, and four years later Jack and Felicia were married, ironically just a few weeks after Jack's first wife, Cynthia, married Cliff Robertson.

"It was sheer coincidence," Jack says, "sheer coincidence. But I always thought we should dig out that barbecue picture and retitle it *Where It All Started*."

Jack and *Felicia Lemmon* are actors, parents, and grandparents. They live in Beverly Hills.

♥♥

Place:
Setting:
Time:

How We Met

_____

_____

_____

_____

_____

_____

_____

_____

_____

_____

_____

_____

_____

About the Author

NANCY COBB lives with her husband and daughter in Guilford, Connecticut.

W9-BIA-150